Boys Will Be Joys

Boys Will Be Joys

DAVE MEURER

SPIRE

© 2002 by David Meurer

Published by Revell
a division of Baker Publishing Group
P.O. Box 6287, Grand Rapids, MI 49516-6287
www.revellbooks.com

New Spire edition published 2011
ISBN 978-0-8007-8800-1

Previously published under the title *You Can Childproof Your Home, but They'll Still Get In.*

Printed in the United States of America.

Scripture marked NIV is taken from the Holy Bible, New International Version®. NIV®. Copyright © 1973, 1978, 1984 by Biblica, Inc.™ Used by permission of Zondervan. All rights reserved worldwide. www.zondervan.com

12   13   14   15   16   17   18   8   7   6   5   4   3   2

For Dad

Acknowledgments

I tip my hat to the usual cast of characters who put up with me through the process of creating this book:

Dale, my lovely, patient, and periodically embarrassed bride.

My sons, Mark and Brad, who each kept saying, "Write about HIM instead of ME!" In an effort to be fair, I took the advice of both (and got twice the material).

Mom and Dad, who let me tell tales (many of which are true) about them.

Steve Laube, my editor, who keeps risking his professional reputation by agreeing to publish my stuff. He *really owes me* for changing my deadline.

Chip MacGregor, who is not ashamed to be called my agent. I suspect a concussion.

Elizabeth, Holly, Alex, Jeanne, Alison, Donna, and all the Bethany House folks who put up with waaaaaay more than they deserve, and who only rarely threaten my bodily person.

The many friends who cheer me on, especially the Memphis troop.

Contents

Introduction

Child development professionals categorize children into two main groups:

(A) Naturally compliant, obedient, well-mannered children
(B) Yours

The implication is rather obvious. If you are blessed with naturally compliant, obedient, well-mannered children, they were accidentally switched at the hospital. But this is not necessarily a bad thing. In a sense, you could look at it as though you won the lottery, and someone else even bought your ticket for you.

Most parents, however, end up with their own children. But don't panic quite yet. Bringing your own children home from the hospital doesn't mean they are destined to be incompliant, disobedient, and ill-mannered, but it does mean that you have to devote massive amounts of time and energy to avoid that outcome. Left to themselves, your children have a natural propensity to be self-centered, pugnacious, and ill-tempered and, if they are boys, wear oversized trousers with enough denim to fashion a Coleman tent.

This book is for all the parents who ended up with their own kids. It is not a professional parenting manual, as I am not a professional. I am just a dad. But I hope that you will find some insight and some helpful tips in my observations, reflections, ruminations, grousings, mutterings, stunned exclamations, incredulous questions, inane outbursts, bulging neck arteries, apologies, failures, and occasional successes.

1

Remember When You Used to Have Dignity?

You are standing in the grocery store checkout line, and right smack behind you stands an enormous biker dude whose vast muscular girth, covered with scary tattoos, is squeezed tightly into a black leather vest. A large gold hoop pierces his right earlobe, a tight red bandana covers his shaved head, and he is pushing a cart full of beverages that would *never* be served at the annual church potluck.

No one dares make eye contact with him.

No one breathes a word to him.

No one . . . except your three-year-old son, who is sitting in your shopping cart and staring in slack-jawed wonder at the sight.

You are praying, *very hard*, that the same angels who stopped the mouths of the lions in the book of Daniel will rapidly intervene before your kid does the thing that, deep down, you *know* he is going to

13

do unless a miracle happens.

The angels are apparently busy elsewhere, because your son drops his box of animal crackers, slowly points his cookie-smeared finger at the biker dude, and squeals, "Dad! Loooooooooooooooook! A pirate!"

> *You are now hurling random wads of cash at the checker, because your short-term goal in life at this point is to get out of that store while your spleen is still in your body.*

You are chuckling nervously and fumbling with your wallet, when your son, wrinkling his nose at the pungent scent of cigarette smoke and motor oil emanating from the shopper, announces, "Dad! That pirate needs a bath!"

You are now hurling random wads of cash at the checker, because your short-term goal in life at this point is to get *out* of that store while your spleen is still in your body.

You scoot your cart into the exit aisle and prepare to make a run for it. Before you get six feet away, your son breaks into a rousing chorus of "Yo, ho! Yo, ho! A pirate's life for me!" (A song that *you* taught him.)

All of the other shoppers who would normally be bellowing involuntary guffaws of merriment are instead biting their lips, or chewing their knuckles, or stuffing an entire eggplant in their cheeks—*anything* to keep from emitting a single giggle.

You sprint, careening your cart toward the parking lot, never looking back.

What do we learn from this experience? Well, we learn that it is unsafe to ever take your young child out into situations where he can possibly come into contact with other human beings, because he will inevitably do something to humiliate you to the point that all your internal organs go into violent spasms and you can only manage to gasp "I'm sorry" to the assorted strangers to whom he has just announced "Watch this" as he proudly shoves his entire index finger up his nose.

One mom told me about a similar experience in a store when she had her young daughter in tow. Both mom and child saw the same shopper at almost the same moment when they rounded a corner into the cereal section.

The sixty-something shopper, probably a very nice grandmother and all-around great American citizen,

You used to have class. Now you have kids. Get used to it.

just so happened to bear an astonishing resemblance to a nasty character in a very popular children's cartoon about a mermaid.

But while the mom was thinking to herself, "Goodness! With that deep purple mascara and silver hair, she looks almost exactly like . . ."

"THE WITCH!!!!!" screamed the daughter, clutching her mom's arm for dear life. "RUN RUN RUN RUN RUN!!!"

"I just wanted to crawl into a hole," recalled the mom ruefully.

You used to have class. Now you have kids. Get used to it.

Dale had our first son, Mark, with her in the store one day when he, then three, was struck with a realization that to him was *way* more important than Einstein's finally figuring out that $E=MC^2$. Earlier in the day, while still at home, Mark realized that he did not know the term for an interesting feature of his body.

"What's this called?" he asked Dale as he pointed to the relevant sector of himself.

So Dale told him.

Pause for several hours, while his little mind processes this information.

Later in the day Dale and Mark were in the grocery check-out line, when Mark's furiously firing neurons finally assimilated and organized the aforementioned information and he came to a logical and, to him, thrilling conclusion:

I have this interesting body feature.

I am like Daddy, but just a smaller version.

So Daddy must have one of these, too!

Shoppers were temporarily blinded as the 9,000-watt incandescent bulb of realization flashed above Mark's head. He beamed with joy, spread his arms wide, and announced to the world, "HEY! MY DADDY HAS A (anatomical feature, edited by publisher, but you can take an educated guess)."

Dale is still recovering from this event, although Mark is now in college.

Even if you wisely choose to never leave home

with your children, this does not mean you can relax.

One day Dale and I woke up to the following sound: *Sklitch. Sklitch. Sklitch.*

Mark discovered, at age two, that eggs are a lot like balls, except they make this great splat on the living room carpet at six in the morning. Neither Dale nor I are morning people, but we soon learned to snap awake and make a flying leap for the kitchen when we heard the refrigerator door open in the morning.

I occasionally have flashbacks, kind of like a combat veteran. We will be staying overnight with friends, and the sweet, thoughtful hostess will get up early in the morning to start breakfast for us while we are all still in bed dreaming, and I'll hear that refrigerator door open and I'll leap out of bed—actually, still asleep—and fly into the kitchen yelling, "Don't you DARE crack one of those eggs!"

And she'll drop the pan and stammer, "Is . . . is . . . oatmeal OK?"

We never get invited back.

Becoming a dad means you get transformed from the healthy, vibrant, intelligent, youthful person pictured in your wedding photo into a twitching, bewildered, sleep-deprived, Play-Dough-smeared creature who looks like the guy in the photo on the post office wall, only less chipper.

I vividly recall the day Dale and I took our kids, still preschool age, to play at the home of another couple, Rex and Janice, who had boys a few years older than ours. As the kids were running around outside, Dale and I were musing aloud about how exhausting little boys can be. I turned to Janice and commented, "Oh, well. You guys lived through it OK. Tell me, when did it start to get easier?"

Janice had the decency to look stunned and even somewhat sympathetic before she fell to the floor in a shrieking fit of laughter.

It *never* gets easier. It gets different, but not easier.

I sometimes wonder why we can't have lives more like the angels. They are smart, strong, and handsome, and there is no evidence indicating that they lose their hair, become exhausted, or get called down to the school office by an unamused campus nurse because one of the little angels stuffed a green bean up his nose on a dare, and it is *really* stuck.

Come to think of it, there *are* no little angels.

Angels don't have kids.

No "owies" to kiss.

No blankets to tuck in at night.

No crayon portraits to hang on the refrigerator.

I guess that's the trade-off.

You can either have a truly perfect body and the ability to fly anywhere on time and for free, with no lost luggage, or you can have kids. (But at least having kids, by definition, means you also get to enjoy

> *You can either have a truly perfect body and the ability to fly anywhere on time and for free, with no lost luggage, or you can have kids.*

the passion and wonder of sex, which not even the Archangel Michael will ever know.)

Oh, one other big benefit of being human: unlike angels, we get second chances.

Lots of them.

2

Oh Yeah? Says Who?

Many parenting manuals that hit the shelves carry with them either the implied or explicit assertion that you, the parent, are doing something wrong. (Hey, why are you picking up a parenting book if everything is going just boffo?)

I have a different theory. I figure that if you are motivated enough to pick up an advice book, you are already doing something right. You are demonstrating care and concern for your kids. That counts for something. So you are already my kind of person. You are actively seeking input about how to better fulfill your calling. You want to raise your kids well. You are investing time and thought into parenting. In reality, that is about 80 percent of the battle right there.

"Love covers a multitude of sins," the Bible tells us. By extension, I believe that love also covers many of the mistakes we make as we flounder around trying to be good parents. So take heart. Parenting isn't like a huge algebra equation, where one little error completely fouls up the entire program and you don't find out about it until the very end when the $258 million NASA probe plows into the surface of Pluto (and it gets charged against *your* insurance because *your* kid was manning Mission Control).

> *In a laboratory, you get to control all the variables. In your home, you are lucky if you get to control the TV remote.*

Parenting isn't a science. That's why you can't neatly replicate success from generation to generation, family to family, and child to child.

In a laboratory, you get to control all the variables. In your home, you are lucky if you get to control the TV remote.

Does this mean there is no overarching framework for successful parenting?

Of course not. It just means that no one has figured out what it is yet.

Peruse the bookstore shelves and you'll find that many parenting books are basically lengthy repudiations of other parenting books. The fact that there are oodles of theories about parenting tells me several things:

- There is disagreement about what actually works.
- Some of these so-called "experts" have the IQ of Cheez Whiz.
- A technique that works with one kid may not work for another.
- Life is messy.

- It is inherently difficult to raise kids, or we wouldn't keep clear-cutting entire forests to print yet another load of books theorizing about how to do it right.
- Many of the parenting experts who have wholesome, high-achieving, wonderful kids are the people who brought home the wrong children from the hospital, so you should ignore their sanctimonious little pontifications.
- It looks like the human race still needs one final, authoritative book to finally settle the manner.
- This is not that book.
- I need an aspirin.
- You need to pray a LOT if you are going to make it as a parent.

There. I hope you feel informed and empowered now, because I certainly don't.

Since so many other books deconstruct someone else's parenting ideas, I figure I might just as well join in the fray.

Since so many other books deconstruct someone else's parenting ideas, I figure I might just as well join in the fray. It won't prove that I'm right, but at least I can feel haughty and superior for a while until someone critiques my opinions into charred little hunks of smoldering NASA slag.

Let's begin our review of the professional literature by analyzing the foundational bestseller published in 1902 by Dr. Angelo J. Cook titled *Shut Up and Go to Your Room*. This influential book persuaded millions of American parents to preserve domestic tranquility by sending their children to their rooms, where they sat quietly until they emerged eighteen years later and invented the Roaring Twenties and mobsters named "Bugsy." So even though the parents obtained some peace and quiet, we cannot count Dr. Cook's parenting theory as a success.

> *Silence is not the grand goal of parenting, although sometimes we parents would gladly trade our entire life savings and perhaps even a couple of internal organs for an afternoon of peace and quiet.*

Silence is not the grand goal of parenting, although sometimes we parents would gladly trade our entire life savings and perhaps even a couple of internal organs for an afternoon of peace and quiet. But in the end, you really aren't keeping them quiet anyway. You are just delaying the noise, which is building up like the floodwaters behind a dam. The dam eventually fails, and then you are facing a cacophony, which may include the jitterbug and very loud stock market crashes. This is not a good outcome, unless you are a mobster boss.

Fast forward to 1947 when Professor Gwendolyn Smelch released an influential volume titled *Just Let Them Do Whatever They Want.* Parents liked this book a lot, as it left them lots of leisure time, which they spent watching a new invention called television. Twenty years later, this resulted in a generation of selfish, cocky, dope-smoking brats who had terrible body odor and gave each other social diseases and took over university administration offices and called police officers pigs and claimed to be the Love Generation. Clearly, just letting kids do whatever they want is much easier than actually parenting, but even Professor Smelch hinted that she may have erred when she penned a follow-up work titled *OOPS!*

The 1960s gave rise to a plethora of parenting manuscripts, all penned by authors who had impressive

> *God gave your kids to you, but He wants them back.*

academic credentials and no children. Theory was really big in the 1960s. All the theories were stupid too. Fortunately, most of these manuscripts were misplaced by the authors, who were so intent on "finding themselves" that they had no idea what hemisphere they were in. Rule of thumb: Anything printed in the 1960s is not worth reading unless the author HATED the 1960s.

Fortunately, some very good parenting books were eventually produced. You can find these books in bookstores, and I encourage you to read some of them someday, long after you have read mine.

But before you get immersed in or confused by what various authors (me included) have to say about fatherhood, please note that the Author of all Authors has written, "Children are a gift from the Lord." He knows all things—including the nature of kids—and He *still* said that.

They can be exhausting, maddening, and irritating—but they are still a gift.

They can be funny, endearing, and lovable—and truly feel like a gift.

They can wrench your soul and break your heart—precisely because they are such a precious gift.

And to top it all off, they are a gift that comes with strings attached.

God gave your kids to you, but He wants them back.

3

Who Needs Birth Control Once You Have a Kid?

It is absolutely amazing to me that any married couple has more than one child. Please do not mistake that statement for some kind of anti-child rant by a zealot for Population Control, Inc., because it is not. Rather, it is a declaration of sheer wonder that any couple manages to engage in another romantic interlude for the immediate two decades following the birth of their first child.

A baby is the most effective form of birth control ever invented.

I believe babies are far smarter than we give them credit. In fact, I think they are downright scheming. Sure, they look all innocent and adorable and helpless, but behind all that sweetness and cooing and drool works the tiny mind of a person who wants all the toys for himself. And the easiest way he can secure that inheritance is to make sure that you and your spouse never have sex again.

27

It was only through diligent, heroic, dedicated effort that I helped Dale conceive a second child. I think we deserve some kind of medal. Against all odds, overcoming colic and night feedings and ear infections and fevers and diapers and trips to the pediatrician and—worst of all horrors—losing the pacifier, Dale and I still managed to engage in passion. We have Brad to show as proof. We think there may have also been an additional romantic evening back in 1992 when the boys were away at camp, but we can't be sure because we spent most of that week overcoming five years of sleep deprivation.

> *A baby is the most effective form of birth control ever invented.*

When God told Adam and Eve to be fruitful and multiply, He never said it would be easy. Fortunately, at least it starts out easy. As newlyweds you can control most of the interruptions. You can disconnect the phone, lock the doors, pull the drapes, and just enjoy God's gift of rapid breathing.

But unlike your phone, you can't disconnect your kid. This is especially true if your kid is nursing. Babies are extremely invasive. They are time consuming. And they could not possibly care less about your plans to do anything that does not include them.

They get hungry at weird times, and patience is not one of their strong points. They indiscriminately relieve themselves whenever and wherever they feel like it. They wail in church. When you are trying to do them a favor and make them feel better by rocking them and patting them on the back, odds are they will barf on you. And then grin about it. Things that would get a civilized person arrested are done with impunity by babies.

And it doesn't end with infancy. Toddlers also get away with all kinds of shenanigans, because we impute innocence to them.

If *you* were in the welcome line at the airport to meet the President of the United States as he stepped off Air Force One, and if *you* swung *your* arm at him with jerky, halting movements and suddenly grabbed the presidential tie and started chewing on it, *you* would be wrestled to the ground by a dozen federal agents. But toddlers get a free pass because everyone thinks they are clueless and cute.

Well, I say that any kid smart enough to get by the Secret Service is definitely smart enough to keep you from having sex. But you don't have to take my word for it. Look at your own experience. If you have a kid, then admit to yourself that you can't even *begin* to count all the times that you and your spouse were contemplating a little round of conjugal fellowship only to be interrupted by the blood-curdling cry of your baby in the next room. You think this isn't *planned*?

But the maddening thing is that your infant doesn't even have to wail to win. You can even be interrupted by his *silence*.

DAD: "Shhhhh. Honey, he's finally out like a light. Why don't you slip into that blue negligee and I'll light a candle."

MOM: "You're right! It *is* quiet. Almost *too* quiet. Do you think he stopped breathing? He's *never* this quiet this early. I read some articles about babies who suddenly stop breathing!"

DAD: "He's fine!"

MOM: "Oh, honey, I just won't be able to relax until we check on him."

And so the amorous couple tiptoes down the hall and listens at the door.

You could hear a pin drop on the carpet it is so silent in that room.

MOM: (Whispering) "Let's get a little closer so we can hear him."

So they sneak up to the crib, and that kid is as quiet as a snowflake. And in the dim glow of the night-light, they can't see whether his rib cage is moving.

So then they panic and gently jiggle him to see if he will make a little noise.

He doesn't.

Rather, he makes a whole big lot of noise.

"WAAAAAAAAAAAAAAAHHHHHH!"

The evening now has all the romantic potential of a kidney transplant.

Some of you are still desperately clinging to the naïve myth that your baby is as pure as the driven snow. You can't imagine that he is smarter than you, and manipulating you like a puppet.

So let me give you more proof of the premeditated treachery.

As a young, childless newlywed couple, you probably enjoyed showering together. This was both fun and romantic, and it would have also consti- tuted a nominal cost savings on the utility bill except for the fact that you stayed in there so long.

But as a parent, tell me if you ever did the following.

Parent A gets in the shower while Parent B stands *outside* the shower holding the baby, who gets handed off to Parent A once the water temperature is just right. Parent A and the baby are having a great time in there just playing with the water and getting all fresh and tidy. When Parent A is done showering, she asks Parent B to step into the shower to again hold the baby while Parent A dries off. Parent B then hands the baby to Parent A, who exits with little happy boy who now wants to nurse. Parent B showers alone, in cold water.

So we have the spectacle of two legally married naked lovers in a steamy shower, passing like ships in the night.

Parent B bursts into tears.

Has anything remotely like this ever happened to you? Of *course* it has! And it has happened to all your friends too. That's why you need to check your phone bill each month. These so-called "helpless little angels" are sharing their best tactics with each other late at night when you finally fall into an exhausted stupor.

In the face of this kind of opposition, it is incumbent on you and your spouse to find creative opportunities to make out when the kid least suspects it. It isn't just about your desire for sensual camaraderie. The future of the planet rests on this. If these babies succeed in limiting us all to one kid, one of these days the Census Bureau is going to count California and find just 100 people. On the plus side, this will really cut down on traffic. But it also spells demographic doom for Social Security.

So really, it is your moral and patriotic duty to spend as many evenings as possible in a secluded Jacuzzi somewhere. It is a high calling, but I have faith in you.

"But *how*, Dave?" you may exclaim. "We have tried and tried, but this kid is too smart for us! The last time we tried to let grandma and grandpa take our baby for the evening, he came down with irritable bowel syndrome and we got paged at the restaurant. And we had to buy brand-new carpeting for grandma and grandpa."

The answer is really quite simple. You have to carve out time for intimate ventures when your kid does not expect it.

For example, schedule a day off and DO NOT LET THE BABY KNOW ABOUT IT.

The husband leaves for work like he normally does, and even announces loudly, "Well, I'm off to work now!"

The baby immediately falls into a deep sleep so that he is prepared to be up all evening when Daddy gets home. The husband then sneaks back into the house, and he and his wife have a great old time of it.

The key is creativity and flexibility. For example, traffic delays can be a blessing in disguise.

Put your thinking caps on, people!

Your marching orders are to be fruitful and multiply, fill the earth, and be subdued about it!

4

Father's Day Ain't Just for Fathers

Father's Day, some years ago . . .

"OK, guys, it's time!" I heard my wife, Dale, whisper to the kids in the kitchen.

The boys bolted into the living room.

"Close your eyes!" Brad said as he grasped my arm and pulled me toward the back door.

"No peeking!" Mark ordered.

"Slow down so I don't trip," I replied as I shuffled blindly to the backyard.

"OK, you can open 'em!" Brad announced with barely contained glee.

I opened my eyes, took in the scene, smiled at them, and said, "Oh, you shouldn't have! Really! A huge cardboard box! I've been wanting one of these!"

"Not the box!" Brad exclaimed, rolling his eyes. "It's what's *in* it!"

"Well, I'm not a mind reader," I replied.

Brad attempted a rebuttal, but Mark stopped him.

"Don't even try it," Mark whispered to Brad. "If you say anything you'll just encourage him."

"Can we make a fort out of the box?" I asked.

"Just open it!" Mark pleaded.

"If we cut it in a circle, we could probably make a huge Frisbee out of it," I mused.

Impatient shouts of "OPEN IT! OPEN IT! I CAN'T TAKE IT ANYMORE!" erupted.

It was my wife.

Parenthetical Observation: Although I love her dearly, my wife is not the most patient woman in the world. One year, for example, I was helping her get Thanksgiving dinner ready and all I did was ask her to clarify where a few things were so I could more expeditiously be of service, and she became downright snippy.

"Dale, you work in the kitchen all the time, so you know exactly where everything is. You can't expect me to memorize all the little nooks and crannies and where you store things," I said defensively.

"All I asked you to do was get the *milk*," she said.

"And all I asked was where it is," I replied.

"*The refrigerator*," she said dryly.

"I *know* that," I said. "But sometimes you keep it on the top shelf and sometimes you put it in the door rack."

"Could you possibly just LOOK for it?" she asked.

"It's a matter of kitchen efficiency," I replied. "If you would have told me exactly where it was, we could have saved precious seconds of preparation time. I could have just reached in to grab it without having to scan all the possible storage sites. A large meal needs to go like clockwork to get everything prepared on time."

"Dave, I have just wasted *two minutes* discussing where we keep the MILK! How much more inefficient can anything possibly be?" she said.

"My point exactly! That was very big of you to admit it," I replied, delighted that she was finally grasping my point (although it was a bit alarming to watch her dig her fingernails into the kitchen counter).

"I'll tell you what," she said slowly. "Just leave the kitchen, and my efficiency quotient will increase by 9,000 percent. At the rate you are 'helping' me, we'll all starve to death."

Sadly, some women are so territorial about their kitchens that they feel threatened if men offer to help. I suspect that is the secret reason why Dale rarely accepts my assistance.

Sometimes, in an effort to respect her sense of space but still be of service, I just sit on the couch in the living room and call out productivity tips as she fixes a several-course meal for visiting guests. I'm not sure how many of my tips actually get through, however. With all those banging pans I can't imagine how she hears a word I say. Dale is a particularly *loud* chef.

But back to the Father's Day gift, which turned out to be a fourteen-foot trampoline.

"Wow! Thanks! This looks like fun," I said, shredding open the box. "It's just too bad you didn't get something that we could *all* enjoy."

"But we can!" squealed Brad. "Me and Mark like it, too!"

"Then that's even better!" I said.

Because I am quite the handyman, we assembled it quickly* and took turns bouncing away.

To avoid any arguments about who was taking too long for his turn, I employed Dale's kitchen timer and set it for ten-minute increments.

A wise father realizes that children need objective standards and impartial treatment or else their sense of justice feels violated.

"The timer is king," I cautioned the boys. "No arguments."

I climbed up on the trampoline and took precisely three bounces before the timer bell went off.

"I barely got up here!" I sputtered.

"Time flies when you're having fun," Mark said.

"You little cheaters! You fiddled with the dial! You can't just—"

"The timer is king," Brad interrupted, holding up his hand to squelch my words. "No arguments."

A wise father needs to watch out for wise guys.

The trampoline turned out to be one of my favorite gifts. It became a complete backyard recreation center. The kids learned to do complicated flips and tricks, they rolled out sleeping bags and

---

*Editor's note: The term "quickly" is used here in relation to geologic time. In that sense, building the Great Pyramids of Egypt also happened "quickly." Because Bethany House Publishers is a Christian firm with a mandate for integrity and honesty, we can't let Dave get away with this shameless mischaracterization of the facts. It took him all afternoon just to figure out that the trampoline fabric was not "wrapping" for the springs. We checked with his wife.

slept on it for most of the summer, hordes of their friends came over to use it, and it even doubled as a launching pad to jump into our above-ground swimming pool.

My favorite use was when we employed it as a family stargazing center. We would turn off all the house lights, throw blankets and pillows on the trampoline, and just watch the sky. On moonless nights we could see the broad ribbon of the Milky Way stretching on for light years. It was a great time to talk about the enormity of God's power. To feel our own smallness. To discuss how, even though our planet is an infinitesimally small dot in the unimaginably large sweep of the universe, God's own Son came not only to visit our planet but also to live among us and even give His own life for us. We may be small, but we are important to God.

> *A wise father realizes that children need objective standards and impartial treatment or else their sense of justice feels violated.*

One night as we discussed the biblical account of Creation, Brad looked skyward and remarked, "You know, this isn't bad for a day's work."

While no fifth grader has ever uttered a greater understatement, we all agreed with his essential point. God's universe is staggeringly impressive, and there is no better place to view it than flat on your back, cuddled up next to the family God has given you.

Even if I never get the chance to bounce on it more than ten seconds, the trampoline has been a great Father's Day gift.

5

Watch Out!
They're Watching!

You will notice that thus far I have discussed fatherhood in the context of raising boys. This is because my children are boys, and I have no experience raising girls. If God has blessed you with girls, and if they are sweet and nice and polite, then I have nothing to say to you other than the fact that I bitterly resent you.*

But whether you have boys or girls, one fact remains constant. Much of your parenting consists of being *watched*, whether you like it or not. Your kids may seem glued to the video-game screen, but they are mostly watching *you*.

As a parent, your life is going to be monitored to the "nth" degree by your kids. And you can't teach them to be one thing when you are another.

When I was a kid, there was a show on TV called something like *Big-Time Sweaty Fake Actors*

---

*But in a kind, Christian sort of way.

Pretending to Be Professional Wrestlers. I watched it regularly. The action was phony and stupid, but it was fun. I hadn't seen TV wrestling in years, until my son Brad turned it on one day shortly after I had relented—after years of beseeching—and signed up for cable TV.

> *Much of your parenting consists of being* watched, *whether you like it or not.*

It was dramatically different from the dumb but innocent stuff I saw back in the '70s.

The first thing I noticed was the wrestlers making obscene gestures to the audience. The women were dressed so skimpily that it almost qualified as pornography. Then the camera panned the audience. You know the big foam hands you see at baseball games: "We're number one"? Well, this was the same, but different.

There was a three- or four-year-old boy in the audience wearing a big foam obscene gesture. I couldn't believe what I was seeing. I looked closer, and the camera zoomed in on the lettering printed on the palm of the foam hand: "Austin 3:16."

I snapped the TV off and canceled cable service.

What kind of dad would take his kid to that kind of "entertainment"?

Just look at the messages:

- Tough guys flip each other off.
- Tough guys are surrounded by nearly naked women who are purely and only sex objects.
- Tough guys mock the Bible and make fun of John 3:16, which is the core message God has for the world.

They interviewed the father who was holding the little boy.

"What does he think of it?" the announcer laughed.

"Oh, he really loves it," replied the dad.

The oaf.

The question is not whether the kid loves it, but WHY he loves it, and SHOULD he be loving it?

The reality is that the little kid loves his dad. He loves being with Dad, and doing what Dad does. If Dad took him fishing, he would love fishing. If Dad took him to the zoo, he would love the zoo. If Dad dresses up in a Nazi uniform and teaches his kid that Jews are bad, the kid will want a uniform too. I have seen a taped interview with a modern-day Nazi. His wife baked a cake and frosted it with a Swastika. Their fifth grader was wearing a Nazi patch on his shirt.

Like father, like son.

Weep for that boy.

Our job is to help our kids love the *right* things. To guide them toward God, toward the good and the noble. To teach right and wrong and honesty and kindness and respect and generosity at the youngest ages.

Jesus had some scary things to say about the fate of people who lead children astray.

"But if anyone causes one of these little ones who believe in me to sin, it would be better for him to have a large millstone hung around his neck and to be drowned in the depths of the sea" (Matthew 18:6).

Whoa.

Does that make you nervous? It does me. It is *supposed* to.

It is a high calling to be a parent. Your kids are literally a divine mission. It is hard work to be a hero, but it is in your job description. Parenthood is not for wimps.

> *It is hard work to be a hero, but it is in your job description. Parenthood is not for wimps.*

If you don't plan on being a good role model, don't have kids. It is as simple as that. Or if you have kids already and you aren't being who you know you need to be, decide to change. Confess to God that you have been failing, and take very practical steps to do things differently. There are tons of resources to help you. Churches. Youth pastors and youth groups. Shelves and shelves of good, practical books.

But before you get overwhelmed with specific parenting advice, let me offer you this observation: If your child knows you love him, and if he knows you are really trying to be who God wants you to be, and if he sees you apologize when you do wrong, and if he sees you loving your spouse, and if he sees you loving him enough to be tough when you have to, you are generally on the right track as a parent.

You will notice I did NOT say, "If you do all these things your kids will turn out great."

There are no guarantees, even if you do *every-thing* right.

The combination of love, involvement, quality time together, moral guidance, and personal holiness guarantees . . . *nothing*, even though you need to do all of the above.

Does it help? Yes. Are you more likely to produce great kids? Absolutely. I am not minimizing the importance of these things.

But if the combination of love, involvement, quality time together, moral guidance, and personal holiness could guarantee success, how come it didn't work with Adam and Eve?

> *There are no guarantees, even if you do everything right.*

Do you think God is up in heaven saying, "If only I had set a better example! If only I had been more involved! I thought I was spending quality time; I tried to love them, but look how they turned out! If I had just trained them up in the way they should go, they never would have departed from it. It's my fault. I'm a failure!"

When all is said and done, your children are free to choose.

You can put in place the structures that make it conducive for your kids to grow and succeed and love God—but they ultimately make their own choices.

If you have tried hard, and your kids nevertheless take a dark path, don't dump on yourself. Pray for them. Never stop caring. But don't beat yourself up because of their choices. And like the Prodigal Son, they may still come back.

Jesus said, "Let the little children come to me, and do not hinder them" (Mark 10:14).

He didn't say "force them to come to me" or

"drag them" or "heap guilt upon them until they come."

If your kids see in you the qualities of love, loyalty, integrity, and honor, and if they see you living out a love relationship with God, they very well may come to God too.

But if you have done all of the above and they still don't come, in my opinion you are, by definition, a good parent.

Even though Adam went his own way, God was and is a good parent.

6

"Dig Me, Daddy!"

I had barely settled into the car with my twelve-year-old son Brad when he flipped on the radio and tuned in a "classic rock" station that was the newest rage at Parsons Junior High School.

"This station has all the coolest new songs," he exclaimed as the familiar tune of "Proud Mary" by Creedence Clearwater Revival erupted from the speakers.

Clearly, the shrewd radio marketing guys had figured out that the term "classic rock" was much more attractive than "baby boomer rock" or "has-been tunes" or "geezerly sounds of the seventies."

"Classic rock" attracted the forty-something crowd, yet the term was sufficiently ambiguous to fool the young and unsuspecting listeners who were not alive when songs of that era were penned by James Taylor, Francis Scott Key, and Christopher "Motown" Columbus. As far as the junior highers knew, these songs were produced last week.

I smiled as Brad nodded in sync with the beat.

This was *my* music. *Cool* music. I grew up on this stuff. I felt an urge to get up and boogie.

Almost unconsciously, I began to sing along.

"Rollin', rollin', rollin' on the river..."

> Becoming uncool is a measurable process, in the same way that the explosion of the Hindenburg was a measurable process.

Brad's head snapped toward me at roughly twice the speed of an F–16 on full afterburners. Horrified dismay radiated from his bulging, melon-sized eyes. There was a painful drop in cabin pressure as he sucked all the available oxygen into his lungs. His twitching, seventh-grade fingers lunged at the radio and snapped the dial back to the "off" position. In the split second of silence that followed, I could actually *hear* his corpuscles quivering.

"What's wrong? I thought you said it was cool," I asked, bewildered.

"Not if *you* like it," he replied.

There are specific moments that stand out with laser-like clarity in the life of all guys:

The day you proposed to your wife.

The birth of your first child.

The day John Elway retired from the Broncos.

And the day you found out you were no longer cool.

Becoming uncool is a measurable process, in the same way that the explosion of the Hindenburg was a measurable process. One moment you are *looking good*! And *feeling fine*! with the taut skin of coolness wrapped around the steel frame of confidence. But a split second later you are reduced to the flapping windbag of disaster, crashing into the hard tarmac of uncoolness.

It is not an easy landing. And it is always shocking.

Not only are you uncool, but people (typically, your kids) are actually shielding their heads and running for cover lest they be smitten by the flaming debris of your cool-lessness.

You have not merely lost your coolness, you have become the Chernobyl of uncoolness, radiating deadly uncoolness rays as far as Finland.

Not only did Brad turn off the radio, he asked me to drop him off two blocks away from his school.

"I don't want people to see me getting a ride," he said, not adding the painfully logical ending words "*with you.*"

So what's up with all this?

I mean, one minute you are the coolest guy in the world to your kids. They wait in barely containable expectation for you to get home from work so you can wrestle with them and play on the floor.

"Daddy, come and chase me!" they will shriek at the park, oblivious to the scores of other kids and moms and dads sharing a day in the sun.

They will give you a big kiss and a hug goodbye when you drop them off at school. They draw crayon portraits of you to hang on the refrigerator, because you are Super Dad, the Coolest of the Cool!

As the years march on, through camping trips and ball games and assorted adventures, you are the guy your kids most want to be with and emulate.

Your music is the cool music. Your clothes are the cool clothes. Your life is the cool life.

And then one day—*KABOOM!*—it is all over. Not only do your kids know it, but your wife insists on putting sunscreen on your bald spot before you go to the lake.

BALD SPOT?

> *The worst thing you can do is make a desperate, pathetic attempt to reclaim your lost coolness.*

You have basically two options the day you find that you are no longer cool. The first option is to gather up your dignity, make a stiff upper lip, and quietly sell your kid to the circus. However, in many states this is illegal, so you may need to visit a law library to check it out. Your other option is to accept the reality that the baton of coolness has somehow mysteriously passed to another generation. You didn't deliberately hand it off. You didn't even hear the pounding of the feet coming up behind you. You just felt a rush of wind blow by you as the coolness was snatched from your hand.

The *worst* thing you can do is make a desperate, pathetic attempt to reclaim your lost coolness. We have all seen guys try to do this, and it is not a pretty sight. Some guys will go on a spending spree, buying fast cars and bad toupees. Some wear absurdly tight-fitting Speedo swimwear at the beach, apparently hoping that mere fabric will turn them into Olympic-class athletes, when in reality they look as though their sagging bodies have been jammed into toddler underwear.

This is so sad. And it never works. These guys just get silly or, worse, pathetic, or still worse, *vile*.

If you can weather the initial shock of uncoolness, this new status actually carries a significant benefit: humility, which is a bona fide spiritual gift.

Anything that takes your pride and self-centeredness down a notch or two is probably a good thing. Face it, guys, we are far too self-absorbed. Keeping the right "look" tends to seize a lot more of our time and attention than keeping the right "heart," even though God is quite emphatic that the heart is what He is interested in. Uncoolness can open the door to humility and help us realize the biblical truth that our life here is but a vapor. It can reorient us toward the important and eternal, and away from the petty, temporary stuff that occupies us way too easily.

If uncoolness can do all that for us, then uncoolness is actually pretty cool.

7

The Really *and* Truly *New and Improved Paradigm for Parenting!*

Anytime some parenting guru comes up with a radically new theory for how to do parenting right, you should run for cover before you get mugged by the kids who grew up under the new theory. There was nothing new under the sun when Solomon wrote Ecclesiastes, and not much has changed since then. Sure, we have all kinds of new toys and technology, but we still have the same hearts and souls that humanity has possessed for eons. Human nature has not changed. That's why raising kids is still hard.

That said, I do have my own paradigm for parenting. After years of searching for just the right formula, I have narrowed it down to this: "Just wing it."

Before all the child-development professionals

start writing enraged letters to my publisher, let me explain what I do and do not mean.

When I say "Just wing it," I do not mean "Ignore the time-tested, collective wisdom of parents through the ages," nor do I mean that we dismiss revealed truth and substitute our uninformed opinion or the fad of the day. On the contrary, I am a big believer in the concept that the best way to gauge what will work in the future is to see what has worked in the past.

> *After years of searching for just the right formula, I have narrowed it down to this: "Just wing it."*

When I say that we should wing it, I mean that no rule book can possibly cover all the bases, because this ain't baseball; there are no bases to cover—or if there are bases, they are disguised as something else and they also keep moving. Sports have rules for every eventuality. But parenting demands wisdom, flexibility, and continuous course corrections, because God, in His infinite creativity, has ensured that each of your kids is unique. Children, even in the same family, can be as different as night and day, or penguins and aardvarks, or Switzerland and the carburetor off a 1952 Oldsmobile, or Cheez Whiz and Senator Kennedy, or . . . you get the idea.

One kid may be daring and brash, while another is cautious and shy. One kid can be generous to a fault, and one may be selfish or miserly. One may harbor a very early ambition to be a fireman, while his younger brother wants to be a trial lawyer, in which case you *are* a wretched failure and you ought to go stick a bag over your head.

The point is that these very different kids may need very different parenting approaches. Some needs are constants that all kids must have in order to thrive—like love, encouragement, acceptance, guidance, quality time, and broccoli. But your kids are probably different to the point that you need to become a student of their nuances.

There are some truly absurd "programs" out there, claiming to literally be God's personally approved way of raising kids, and which lay down a host of rules that even cover *when* you are supposed to feed your infant so that he will learn to eat God's way. I think that is just plain foolish.

Our youngest son, Brad, was an "easy" baby, whereas Mark was a "hard as triple-plated titanium" baby. Brad slept so soundly that you could have set off an air-raid–warning siren under his crib and the most he would do is yawn. Mark, on the other hand, would snap out of a deep sleep if he so much as heard you THINK the word *sex*, much less actually rustle any sheets.

If Brad got cranky and tired, we could rock him a few minutes, lay him down, and he was zonked out for the night. When we put Mark down for a nap, he would stand up in his crib, grip the bars, and unleash a barrage of infant invective that was so livid, so angry, and so intense that it was clearly the baby version of cussing us out. A platoon of Marines would have flinched if they'd heard Mark at age one. I'm just thankful he didn't know any actual words. Mark would do this for what seemed like *forever*, until sheer exhaustion conked him out.

Dale and I would sit in the living room and quiver, wondering what we had done wrong.

But these differences in our boys had ZERO to do with anything we did as parents. They were like this from day one.

Mark had an affinity for drawing even as a very young child, and he has blossomed into quite an artist. Brad is not interested in sketching, but he's into the guitar. Of course, the boys also share some common interests, such as hitting me up for money, mocking my bald spot, and lunging for my car keys unless I remember to lock my key ring in a vault.

But my boys are very different from each other, and the odds are that your kids are not carbon copies of each other, either.

Mark was the original strong-willed child. When Mark was three, Dale joined a cooperative preschool, where the moms took turns assisting the main teacher, Mrs. Pat. One day Mrs. Pat pulled Dale aside and commented, "You know, Mark does not so much *play* with the other children as he *organizes* them into little work groups so they will build the building blocks his way."

It was true. We watched him. He was a miniature general contractor, clearly frustrated by the substandard skill level of his pathetic laborers.

"Put THAT block there and THIS one here or you have to LEAVE," he barked at one member of the crew.

It was a long and difficult process to get Mark to agree to allow the other little children to make building block structures in what he termed the "wrong way."

Brad, on the other hand, was Mr. Mellow. He deferred to other kids, liked to share toys, and happily participated in group activities, while Mark stood on a chair to put the finishing touches on a scale model of the Empire State building that was only slightly smaller than the real thing.

Same gene pool, different kids. Same parents, but each kid requiring a different approach.

A sculptor studies a block of marble before working on it. A jeweler examines the hunk of rock before he cuts out a gem. We parents are like those artists,

> *Our kids are not widgets or robots or computer programs that predictably react to our "input."*

the main difference being that marble can sit still for more than fourteen seconds, and emeralds don't belch at the table.

But like sculptors, we need to study our kids and see their sometimes subtle differences before we set about the task of shaping and molding their lives.

The Bible speaks of believers as "living stones" that are being built into a temple for God. I think that is an apt metaphor for parenting. Our kids are not widgets or robots or computer programs that predictably react to our "input." They are living stones.

Of course, the comparison breaks down, because God is all-powerful, which is an extremely helpful attribute when you are dealing with living stones.

Fortunately, God does not require you to make

an entire temple out of these squirming, scampering, bouncing, and, eventually, *driving* stones. He is asking that you do your level best to set them on a solid foundation. Then He will do the heavy lifting.

8

Faith of Our Fathers

And without faith it is impossible to please God.
—Hebrews 11:6

It is a bright and unusually balmy Friday afternoon in late October, but I am not taking a walk outside. I am sitting in a small waiting room as my youngest son, Brad, slowly emerges from the haze of the anesthetic.

The swimming pool into which he took a flying leap had a shallow end much more shallow than he expected. Fortunately, he did not dive in. He went in feet first, and crunched his knee a good one.

Dale and I were with him as the medical staff began running drugs through a tube and into his veins. He grinned a dopey, sleepy smile as the first wave hit him.

We stayed until he was conked out, and the nurse steered us out of the room.

I am sitting in the waiting room tapping keys on a laptop computer. I am doing this not because

I am a workaholic or on a deadline, but because I am nervous and I either occupy my fingers with a keyboard or I flip the pages of a waiting room magazine with a headline that blares "Ike Wins Second Term."*

I told Brad, truthfully, that this was a minor surgery and he should be up and around in no time.

What I did not tell him was that the dark and ugly word DEATH kept assaulting my mind. Yes, it was extreme and overblown and borderline irrational. But sometimes patients have unexpected adverse reactions to anesthesia, or a technician makes some huge error, and what was supposed to be a minor outpatient procedure becomes a stunning tragedy.

And so parents worry.

Call it stupid.

Call it a lack of faith.

Call it common.

I am not excusing it, I am just confessing that it is a reality. We worry about our kids because we love them so much.

I could probably come up with a good euphemism for the word *worry*, perhaps substituting *concern* or *uneasiness* to kind of scoot by Jesus' admonition against worrying, hoping He won't notice. After all, He never specifically said we can't be *concerned* or *uneasy*. But those are word games.

I'm worried.

Parents worry.

---

*What IS IT with hospital waiting rooms? Is there some federal law mandating that we be spared any dangerous exposure to current events?

Any parent who says he doesn't worry about his kids is not being honest, or is kidding himself.

We are called to faith. But worry comes naturally, and faith does not. Worry is our default position. Worry is easy. Faith is hard. Faith is mysterious.

Faith worries me.

I know, I am pathetic. That's why I need a savior. I am banking on enormous doses of forgiveness even as I try to get a handle on this thing called faith.

I think worry can be a door to faith. We worry, so we pray. That seems like a step toward faith. So maybe I am in the middle of a normal progression toward faith.

But faith in *what*, exactly? "Faith" that things will all turn out well? "Faith" that Brad will be fine?

No.

I can *hope* that things will turn out OK. I can *pray* that Brad will be fine. But can I be confident of the outcome?

> *I think worry can be a door to faith. We worry, so we pray. That seems like a step toward faith.*

No.

There are no guarantees that I will get what I pray for.

Life is full of bad events, and these events seem randomly distributed throughout the world with no discernible rhyme or reason. I have several friends who are walking around with cancer. It is dormant right now, but it could take off like a rocket at any time. I have friends who have lost children to the cruel and icy hand of death. I have friends who have suffered in almost unimaginable ways.

And yet we are called to faith.

Not faith in a specific outcome. But faith in a specific person.

Faith in God.

But what does it mean to have faith in God when your kid is in the hospital, or your spouse has a strange lump, or someone who was too young to die has just died?

I have no faith in outcomes.

I have no faith in the future.

I have no confidence that things will happen the way I hope and pray they will.

But I trust in God.

I trust that He is good, even when circumstances are not.

I trust Him when He says that someday He will wipe away every tear from our eyes.

I trust that when He chooses not to give me the answer I want, He is wise.

I trust that He has His reasons for what He does and what He *permits* in this fallen, wretched world that is filled with so much pain and suffering.

And I have faith that He will forgive me for my lack of faith.

> *Immediately the boy's father exclaimed, "I do believe; help me overcome my unbelief!"*
> —Mark 9:24

9

On the Road Again

It didn't seem like a dangerous idea at the time.

Because my "day job" periodically requires a significant amount of time away from home, I decided to look for opportunities to allow my boys to take turns traveling with me on appropriate occasions.

SPECIAL NOTE TO UNITED STATES JUSTICE DEPARTMENT: Yes, I pay for any extra costs incurred by my kids, including the twenty-seven sodas.

One time I was invited to speak to a trade group in Reno, Nevada, about federal forest policy. Although the city of Reno thrives on gambling, it also boasts one of the most spectacular classic automobile collections in the nation. I approached my son Mark, then thirteen, about going with me.

"There are pros and cons," I explained to Mark. "On the plus side, we'll stay in a nice hotel with a huge pool, and we'll eat like kings, and we'll spend Saturday afternoon looking at some of the coolest cars on the entire planet."

"What's the bad news?" he asked cautiously.

"First, you'll have to miss an entire day of school. Second . . ."

A deafening sonic boom drowned out my words and shook family photos off the wall as Mark roared into his room at 800 miles per hour, where he commenced hurling socks and shirts into his gym bag at a speed measured in nanoseconds.

"There is an educational component to this trip!" I called down the hall. "You'll have to sit through some lectures about things that probably don't interest you very much."

"Then it will be just like home," he replied.

Har-dee-har.

As we cruised into the gambling haven, we noticed signs advertising "exotic dancers" and "gentlemen's clubs."

It was seedy and sad, but it gave us the opportunity to talk about the difference between love and lust, about respect for women, and about the dynamics that would drive a young woman to seek employment in the sordid world of strip clubs.

> *It was a significant teaching moment—a moment that may not have naturally arisen had we not been traveling together.*

"There has to be a lot of heartbreak, humiliation, and desperation in the lives of those girls," I mused.

"Yeah," Mark agreed somberly. "No one ever thinks about that."

By talking about these "exotic" women in the context of someone's daughter or sister, and conjecturing about their histories and their lost dreams, they became objects of prayer instead of dehumanized sex objects. It was a significant teaching moment—a moment that may not have naturally arisen had we not been traveling together.

We got to the hotel, endured a series of speeches (including mine), went swimming, saw the cars, and generally had a great time.

But the trip had an unintended consequence.

When we got home, I overheard Mark explaining to a friend that my job largely consisted of swimming at hotels and going to car shows.

"He also gives some speeches, and everyone has to clap because he is from the government. I think it's a law," Mark explained.

I tried to correct this horribly flawed assessment, but by some odd coincidence one of my next weekend duties consisted of helping to judge the "Kool April Nites" car show in our hometown.

Of course, both my sons wanted to go. They also wanted to bring friends.

Even though I was doing this on a weekend, on my own time and on a voluntary basis, the rumor mill began churning among the gang of boys.

"So this is what your dad does for a *job*?" whispered one kid as we all examined a 1957 Chevy Bel Air with flames painted on the front fenders.

"Well, it isn't *all* he does," Mark corrected. "Sometimes he has to go to free dinners."

"Hey, just a minute," I protested. "It isn't all fun and games. Sometimes the chicken breasts are a bit overcooked and dry. There is also the real danger of getting served non-dairy powder instead of real cream for coffee."

They were unsympathetic.

One day I dragged in the door at home after a full day at the office, where I had cranked out volumes of paperwork on a deadline about a major issue.

> *Mark looked up at me, concern etched on his brow, and asked, "Tough day at the buffet?"*

Mark looked up at me, concern etched on his brow, and asked, "Tough day at the buffet?"

The downside of taking your kid with you to work is that the short snippet they observe about your occupation may create an erroneous impression about what you actually do day in and day out. But I still recommend it, mostly because as the adult you can still ground them if they get too cheeky.

For many parents, occasionally taking your kid to work is not an option. But even if you can't take your kids on the road or to your job site, you can and should take the opportunity to educate them about exactly what it is you do to put food on the table. They need to understand that part of your life.

For those of you who can occasionally bring your kids into your work world, I suggest you do. Just being in a different context, away from home, can open up new opportunities to communicate, teach them about the world of work, have some fun, and bond. However, I also suggest that you try to periodically do something ordinary, so your kids see the routine and mundane aspects of work. Lastly, and this is critically important, make sure you hit the buffet line that has the beef. The chicken is almost always lousy.

10

"Deadline" Is Not Just Another Word for "Whenever"

At the beginning of Mark's last year in high school, parents of seniors were asked to attend a meeting in which teachers would explain the rules and deadlines governing the mandatory, and dreaded, "senior project."

"I cannot stress how important this is," the teacher said. "Students *cannot* graduate without completing this task. It is a significant undertaking and will require significant amounts of time. It is *imperative* that your seniors work on this project throughout the year, because there simply is *not time* to throw it together at the very end of the second semester. If your student does *not* complete this project, he or she will assuredly *fail* high school and ruin his or her entire future and end up doing menial labor in a grim, dark warehouse run by former Soviet Union prison guards."

Well, she didn't exactly say that last part, but that is how all the parents translated it as we sat there twitching in fear. Because the REAL message was that we, too, had a senior project—making sure that our senior finished his project. Our mission impossible, regardless of whether we chose to accept it, was to force our chronically and habitually procrastinating offspring to get this project done on time, or die trying.

> *Our mission impossible, regardless of whether we chose to accept it, was to force our chronically and habitually procrastinating offspring to get this project done on time, or die trying.*

"The first deadline is September 24, at which time your student *must* turn in a preliminary idea, which *must* be approved by the supervising instructor," continued the teacher. "You are now excused, and may God have mercy on your souls."

We exited the classroom like a herd of nervous cattle.

"So, Mark, what do you think you want to do for a project?" I asked as we drove home from the meeting.

"I don't know. I have a few weeks to think about it. I want to do something interesting and different," he replied.

"Well, just don't let the time get away from you," I cautioned.

"No sweat. October 24 is a long way off," he said.

"THAT'S SEPTEMBER 24!" I roared.

"Whatever," Mark replied serenely.

Every few days either Dale or I would casually question Mark about his project concept.

"I have other homework I have to do right now, but I'll get to it," he would inevitably reply.

There is a school of thought out in parent land that goes like this: "By the time your kid is a high school senior, you need to let him sink or swim on his own. Good grief, he is going to turn eighteen sometime in his senior year, which will make him a legal adult. You should not be doing any hand-holding or cajoling or worrying. It is his life, and his responsibility, so let him rise to the occasion. Just let go. If he fails, it is up to him. He has to learn about the real world. How can he grow up and take responsibility if you are hovering over him like he was eight instead of eighteen?"

But there is a second school of parental thought that goes like this: "If he does not graduate, he will live with us forever. 'GET OFF YOUR SLOTH-FUL BACKSIDE AND GET THAT PROJECT DONE!!!' "

And there is a final school of parental thought that goes like this: "The teen brain does not actually finish forming until age thirty-two. Concepts like 'cause and effect' are clearly beyond them, as exhibited by the panic that ensues when the student discovers he has no clean clothes to wear and he must be at school in ten minutes."

"I don't have any clean clothes!" the student will yelp.

"That's because they are all dirty and in a huge

wad in the corner of your room exactly where you left them, and clothes do not carry themselves to the hamper where, had they been deposited in the first place, they would have been washed with all the other laundry as we have discussed on several dozen occasions," the mother will reply.

"But I don't have any clean clothes!" the student will reply.

I have enrolled in all three of these schools of thought, hopping from theory to theory based upon what strikes me at the moment. What I lack in consistency I make up for in yelling. There are occasions when Dale and I just allowed the logical consequences to flow, but that was after we first tried to help the kids understand the potential outcomes.

> *What I lack in consistency I make up for in yelling.*

For example, Mark is an extremely sound sleeper. We bought him an alarm clock so he could get up on time for school, but he would often snooze right through it or turn it off and go back to sleep. So we bought him two alarm clocks and advised him to set them in far corners of his room so he would have to actually get up to turn off the incessant buzzing.

It was no good. He was relying on me to come in and whack him on the head with a pillow before he would get up.

I finally told Mark I was drawing a line in the sand. He needed to set his alarms, get up, and be ready to go by 7:15 A.M., when I was taking Brad to school, or I would simply leave without a word and he could walk the few miles to school and be tardy and be required to take "Saturday school classes," to which I would also make him walk.

If that isn't an ultimatum, what is? But I felt it was a legitimate, logical, rational way to drive home the point that he had to start growing up in this area of his life.

"The key is follow-through," I told Dale as we climbed into bed. "It is more important that he learns this lesson than it is to get him to class on time. Besides, after one day of walking the lesson will be learned."

"It is also important that you don't chew him out," Dale advised. "If this is going to be about logical consequences, then don't muddy the waters by injecting your own emotion into it. That changes the subject and makes it a conflict between you and Mark rather than a conflict between Mark and the reality that the world won't bend itself to his schedule. This will only work if we stay calm."

"Right. So we are agreed," I said.

"Well, right. But just remember to keep your cool," Dale said. "You know how you get."

"Nonsense, my sweet!" I replied. "I shall be the very picture of patience and reserve. Besides, I think we made an impression on him. He'll probably be wide awake long before dawn."

The next morning . . .

7:00 A.M. Brad was dressed and finishing breakfast. There was not the slightest sound
from Mark's room.

7:03 A.M.   I strolled by Mark's room and coughed loudly. Dale arched an eyebrow at me—a silent reminder to just let the consequences flow.

7:09 A.M.   I was sipping my morning coffee, my white knuckles wrapped in a death grip around the hot mug of brew, trying to not shout down the hall.

7:11 A.M.   I was chewing viciously on a piece of toast, and saying in an unusually loud voice, "So, Brad, it looks like you are all ready to GO TO SCHOOL in a couple of minutes!" Dale shook her head slowly.

7:14 A.M.   I bolted down the hall to Mark's room, pounded on the door and shouted, "We are leaving without you! This is completely irresponsible! You have ONE MINUTE TO GET READY!" I vexed and frothed and bellowed and generally gave my cardiac system a great workout in the ensuing sixty seconds as Mark threw on his clothes and grabbed his books and flew out the door carrying his shoes and socks. I then barked and howled like a wounded bloodhound all the way to school.

I was still a seething, muttering, twitching wreck when I got back home.

"Dave, that wasn't exactly according to plan," Dale noted as I finished getting ready for work. "How is he going to take us seriously if we don't follow through? He has to learn to be on time, and you are actually preventing him from learning because you keep bailing him out."

I wanted to argue, but she was right. I had blown it.

So I sat Mark down when he got home and explained, at enormous length, that the ball was now in his court. He *had* to get himself up and be ready to go or he would walk to school and get the tardy slip and go to Saturday school. There would be no second chances. If he was late, he alone would pay the price.

"Is that really what you want?" I asked.

"No," he said. "I'll really try."

The next day...

7:00 A.M. Brad was dressed and finishing breakfast. There was not the slightest sound from Mark's room.

7:03 A.M. I strolled by Mark's room and listened, but said nothing.

7:09 A.M. I was sipping my morning coffee, my white knuckles throttling the cup, but I said nothing.

7:11 A.M. I was chewing on my lip instead of my cold toast.

7:15 A.M. Brad and I left for school.

I prayed on the way back home. Prayed for Mark. Prayed for patience. Prayed for wisdom as we tried to do what was in Mark's best interest in the long term.

On my way back home I passed Mark as he trudged to school, backpack full of books on his shoulders, head hanging down.

The next day...

Mark slept in again. When he got home, he complained that we didn't wake him up. I bit my lip.

The next day...

Mark was still asleep when we left.

The next day...

He made it. The angels rejoiced, the Red Sea parted, captives were set free, the mountains broke into shouts of joy, and the parents were delivered from the hand of the oppressors.

But back to the senior project.

It was the evening of September 23 when it suddenly occurred to Mark that he needed to have a senior project proposal turned in the next morning.

We were having dinner when Mark suddenly went white in the face and spluttered, "I have to turn in my senior project proposal tomorrow!"

"I'm shocked! Stunned! Bewildered! How could they spring this on you with no warning?" I said.

> We were having dinner when Mark suddenly went white in the face and spluttered, "I have to turn in my senior project proposal tomorrow!"

Mark was up until the wee hours of the morning doing Internet research and putting together a proposal to write a paper on the history of mural painting and to also paint a mural incorporating the stylistic techniques of Vincent van Gogh.

He was exhausted, but he met the deadline.

"Well, did you learn anything from this little

episode?" I asked when he dragged in from school.

"Yeah," he said. "I work best under pressure."

The hospital orderlies had to sedate me before they could strap me to the gurney.

The months rolled inexorably forward, with the senior project looming over us like a mighty volcano ready to detonate.

I will spare you the agonizing details, but suffice it to say that there were two weeks left in the semester when Mark suddenly realized that he had an enormous mural project due.

"I have an enormous mural project due!" were his exact words.

"I have an enormous mural project due!" were his exact words.

"No! It can't be!" I replied.

"I need paint! I need brushes! I need a big sheet of plywood! I need a conceptual drawing!" he cried. "We don't have any of the supplies I need! Why don't you and Mom keep basic supplies on hand, like tubes of acrylic yellow?"

Despite Dale's very good advice to the contrary, I launched into a long and blistering lecture.

"Try getting away with this in the real world! You'd be fired in a moment! The rest of the world is not going to wait around for Mark Meurer as he fritters away his time and plays around and leaves important projects until the last minute! This is completely irresponsible! Lack of planning on your part does not constitute an emergency on my part! It is time to start acting your age, young man!"

Mark threw himself into the project almost nonstop, drawing and painting for hours on end. He would paint from the minute he got out of school until one or two o'clock in the morning, then drag himself to school, and then repeat the grueling process the next day.

He was still putting the last touches on it fifteen minutes before it had to be loaded on a truck and hauled to the school for judging.

He got an A.

"See? It went fine," he grinned.

Dale stuffed a sock in my mouth and made me go lie down.

Because I had been so consumed with Mark's project, I had slipped behind on one of my own deadlines for a manuscript that was due at the publisher in a few short weeks.

I was furiously typing away later that evening, well into the night, when Mark walked into my office.

"You look stressed," he observed.

"Oh, I'm just a little behind on this book," I replied.

"Dad, haven't you known about this deadline for months? This is completely irresponsible! The world is not going to wait for Dave Meurer to decide whether or not deadlines mean anything," he cackled gleefully.

"I don't need this right now," I said through clenched teeth.

"Sorry," Mark said. "Is there anything you need

right now that I can get for you?"

"Thanks. You could make me some coffee," I said.

"You didn't make coffee yet? Lack of planning on your part does not constitute an emergency on my part," he chortled, messing up my hair and tickling me.

The problem with young people today is that they refuse to learn from their elders.

|| 11 ||

On the Road Yet Again

And then there were the trips with Brad.

Our first overnight business trip included a late evening meeting. I knew it would be a long night, so we arrived early enough to get in some exercise at the motel pool.*

After swimming, I gave Brad the choice of places to go for dinner.

"Cheap burger and fries, or a steak and potato?" I asked.

"Like, at a nice place?" he replied.

"Yep. There's a steak place right next door," I said. "But you have to use excellent manners."

He decided good manners would be a small price to pay for a steak dinner. It was the choice I was hoping he would make. I wanted to test how my eleven year old would comport himself with white linen tablecloths.

---

*The author prefers an exercise regimen that does not involve sweating. Or, if sweating is absolutely *required*, the author figures that the best place to experience it is someplace where you won't, in fact, experience it. Clearly, the author has no intention of taking up jogging.

The waitress seated us at a cozy booth with a small oil lamp glowing on the table, dimly illuminating far more utensils per person than Brad was used to.

"What's with all the forks?" Brad asked.

"The small one is for your salad, the larger one is for your meal, and the sideways one at the top of your plate is for the dessert you are not going to have because we won't have time before we have to get to the meeting," I said.

"Three forks is stupid," he whispered.

Brad looked at me with the same expression he would have adopted if his teacher asked him to name the capital of Uzbekistan.

"True, but it is nevertheless the rule," I said. "Touch the wrong fork at the wrong time and the sirens go off. Just play along. Have you decided what you want?"

"Just order something for me," he whispered.

"You'll do fine," I said.

The waitress arrived before Brad could challenge that assertion.

"Have you had time to decide?" she asked with a smile.

I nodded at Brad.

"I'll have the steak," he said politely.

"How do you want it?" she asked.

Brad looked at me with the same expression he would have adopted if his teacher asked him to name the capital of Uzbekistan.

I had never in his entire life asked him how he wanted his meat cooked, mostly because I, as master of the barbecue, always made that executive decision based upon how safely I could approach the bellowing conflagration and—shielding my eyes— plunge a fork blindly into the inferno until something vaguely cow-like came out.

Reading his puzzled brow, she asked, "How would you like it cooked?"

Brad sighed with relief.

"Like my mom makes it."

"And how would that be?" she asked, still smiling.

"Good."

I stepped in.

"Brad, what do you want it to look like?"

"Pink on the outside and black on the inside," Brad grinned, folding his menu.

All in all, it was a big success in learning about how to dine in an upscale establishment.

On another occasion, when Brad was fifteen, I pulled him out of school for a day to attend a congressional field hearing regarding the extremely dangerous and addictive drug methamphetamine, which has become a major problem in California. It was a long but powerful day, filled with gritty testimony from recovering addicts, narcotics agents, and district attorneys. We heard horrific stories of infants and children who were raised in "homes" that doubled as makeshift labs filled with toxic fumes and residues from cooking chemicals. The fortunate kids were rescued and placed in foster homes when the police busted the labs. Other kids were killed when the lab exploded. Some were tortured and murdered by their parents or the assorted

strangers who move in the dark world of drug dealing.

It was a pretty heavy day for both of us. Maybe
too heavy? I don't know.

My wife and I have tried to walk that delicate
balance between shielding our kids from the worst
of life, while also exposing them, at appropriate
ages, to the life lessons that can best be learned by
getting up close and personal with the ragged effects
of sin. It is not an easy balance. And they see far
more of the seedy side of life than we wish they
would, simply because it is everywhere.

I am tempted to get kind of whiny here about
how hard we have it as modern parents as we try to
raise kids in a society that increasingly seems to
assault everything decent and noble. I mean, it *is*
hard—but do we honestly have it any harder than
the moms and dads who lived in, say, Rome or Cor-
inth a couple thousand years ago? Those places were
home to a culture that was filled with open prosti-
tution (in some places it was part of the religion!),
graphic and often lethal violence for entertainment
(ever hear of gladiators?) and open infanticide that
barely raised eyebrows.

We get incensed—legitimately—about the trash
that passes for "entertainment" on TV, at the movies, and in music. But ancient cultures were likewise
immersed in junk. There is no way to shield our
kids from the trash of the world. It hangs like a fog
in the air. I think our task is to help them see it as
God sees it. To develop His heart, His compassion,
and His view of the world so that, like Jesus, they

can move among the temptations of life without embracing the darkness.

There is no formula for doing this. You will teach them in a thousand different ways in a thousand different contexts as you do stuff together and live out your own faith before them.

In the big scheme of things, Brad was right. Three forks *are* stupid. What really matters is the fork in the road, and what path your kids choose when you can no longer walk it with them.

‖ 12 ‖

Good Job!

"Dad, can you take me to apply for a job?" asked Brad, newly sixteen.

I glanced at his fashionable interview attire, consisting of a T-shirt, board shorts, and sneakers with untied laces.

"Do you want to just apply for a job, or actually get one?" I replied.

"Huh?"

"No employer is going to hire you if you're dressed like a beach bum," I said.

"But I'm applying at Jamba Juice. Everyone there wears shorts and a T-shirt," Brad noted.

"They may let you dress that way once they hire you, but trust me, the boss will take you more seriously if you dress professionally for the interview," I said.

"When you say 'professionally,' you don't mean like *you*, do you?" he replied with raw panic in his voice. "I don't want to look like a dork!"

"And just what is *that* supposed to mean?" I snorted.

"It's not an insult," Brad replied, rushing to repair the damage. "I mean, see, it's OK for you to dress like a dork because everyone expects it, but there's no way that I—"

"Thanks for clarifying that," I interrupted. "And just what is wrong with the way I dress?"

Brad glanced down at my polished burgundy wing-tipped shoes.

"Well, for starters—" he replied.

"Never mind!" I snapped. "The point is that the person doing the hiring is not going to be a teenager. It will be someone who dresses like me, and we dorks like to hire other people who dress like dorks. Trust me on this."

> *"Do you want to just apply for a job, or actually get one?"*

"I'll wear a dress shirt, not tucked in, and no tie," he offered.

"You'll look like Oscar Madison," I replied. "You need a dress shirt, tucked in, with a tie, and I'll even loan you my wing tips."

That last part was purely for shock value, to make the tie seem easy by comparison.

Brad emerged from his room ten minutes later looking very dapper in his black slacks, gray shirt (tucked in), and deep maroon tie.

"You look great," I offered.

"If anyone sees me, I'll move to another town," he replied.

We got in the car and made our way toward the juice bar.

"Have you thought about what to say?" I asked.

"What do you mean?"

"The first question the guy is going to ask you is 'Why do you want to work here?' " I said.

"You can't know what he's going to say," Brad retorted.

"It's standard," I said. "So let's practice your answer."

"I want to earn money," Brad replied.

"Wrong," I said.

"How can it be wrong? That's why anyone wants a job!" Brad replied.

"They already know you want to earn money. But that is a boring and unimaginative answer," I said. "How did you even think to apply at this place? Why didn't you apply somewhere else?"

"Well, I went to a Jamba Juice in Sacramento and I really like their drinks, and it seems like a fun place to work," Brad said.

"Then that's your answer," I said as we drove into the parking lot.

Fifteen minutes later . . .

Brad floated out the door and toward the car.

"I start Wednesday," he said.

"Congratulations!" I said, extending my palm for a high five.

"What was his first question?" I asked.

" 'So, Brad, why do you want to work here?' " Brad grinned.

"So was I right or was I right?" I gloated.

"You were right," he agreed.

"Does the old man know what he is talking about?" I prodded.

"Yeah," Brad acquiesced.

"So, am I one cool dude or what?"

Brad glanced down at my shoes.

"Let's not push it," he advised.

Word travels fast to friends and family that Brad has landed his first real job. Heretofore the jobs have consisted of chores around home, or lawn mowing for the neighbors, or odd jobs for friends and grandparents. Nothing that requires federal withholding tax. Brad has just taken a quantum leap into the adult world.

> *It is the same mix of euphoria and wistfulness that washed over me when they took their first hesitant steps.*

Grandma casually asks me, "So what's it like having both your boys working at real jobs?"

"Great," I reply. "It gives them something to do with their summers; no whining about being bored, and I can hit them up for a loan for little luxuries like food to refill the refrigerator that they strip like locusts every day."

I say the words glibly, and on one level I mean them. But even as I joke around I feel a sinking sensation in my chest. It is the same mix of euphoria and wistfulness that washed over me when they took their first hesitant steps, rode a bike without training wheels, sprouted a faint mustache—they are growing up, and I *know* where this is going, and I don't like it one little bit.

And I do.

And I don't.

And I . . .

Part of me is cheering them on. And part of me

longs deeply for those days I got cramps in my leg from bouncing them in a game of horsey ride. I miss having a grinning, drooling toddler latched to my shin. I would hand you a thousand dollars if I could hear those giggles, and have those leg cramps, one more time.

But that is ancient history now.

Slowly, almost imperceptibly, God has been easing my boys away from me and into independence.

When your kid gets a job, it is a sure sign you are losing yours.

God, I know this is your plan, but I don't like it. But then again, this is great.

13

Intensive Scare Unit

Pastor Jim was distressed as he read the visitation request card. Bob, a pillar of the church and the father of two junior high boys, was not only hospitalized, but lying in the intensive care unit.

Jim scanned the card for additional information, grimaced, and sat down stunned. While it was certainly an unusual procedure for a forty-year-old man, it should not have been remotely dangerous. Something must have gone terribly wrong.

Jim bit his lip as he thought about the family. In fact, Bob's two boys had just spent the night at the church as part of a youth group function. They were still crashed out on the floor of the youth building with all the other kids.

I wonder if they know yet? he thought as he grabbed the phone to call Bob's wife. The odds were that she would be at the hospital, but he would try the home number first.

The phone rang three times before Pastor Jim heard the familiar voice.

"Bob?! You're home already? What happened?" Jim stammered.

"Pastor Jim? What are you talking about?" came the reply.

While it was certainly an unusual procedure for a forty-year-old man, it should not have been remotely dangerous.

"Well, I'm holding a hospital visitation card that says you are in the intensive care unit recovering from, uh, an 'emergency circumcision.'"

There was a long pause as both men did the quick mental calculation:

Boys + overnight access to church office = humiliating prank.

Bob actually maintained his composure pretty well, under the circumcisions. I mean, the circumstances!

When Bob told me this true story, the first fatherly thought that popped into my mind was *Who can I pull this joke on?*

But I had an additional thought as well: *It is neat that Bob's kids felt safe enough to joke around with him like that.* Because although at first they gave someone a bit of a scare, what really scares me is when families don't joke around. I'd much rather see too much sophomoric, silly joking than too little of it.

I periodically meet very dedicated, concerned, serious Christian parents who seem virtually incapable of just letting go with a fit of laughter. I'm not talking about laughing at the bawdy or even remotely morally questionable stuff. I'm talking about good clean jokes, or the banter around a board game, or the silly antics of a child. These are often the people who, deep down, can't imagine Jesus ever laughing.

But it is precisely because life is so serious and the stakes are so high that we need to laugh more. If your

Boys + overnight access to church office = humiliating prank.

kids are trying to joke with you, take it as a gift from God.

Obviously, you need to teach them boundaries and the line between joking around and actually hurting others. That's all part of parenting. Sometimes they will cross the line, and that is when you teach them the difference. But good, clean, fun joking around should be encouraged and fostered.

Unfortunately, sometimes even when you teach them the difference between appropriate and inappropriate joking they don't quite get the point the first time, so you may have to revisit the issue again and again. For example, even though I have emphatically informed my boys that my creeping baldness is never, for *any* reason, an appropriate topic for joking, they keep veering across that double yellow line like an out-of-control tanker truck careening brakeless down a mountain road during an ice storm.

I'll drop Brad off for a haircut and he will offer to sell me the clippings to paste on my forehead. Or I will walk out the door into a beautiful, sunny spring day and Mark will cup his hands over his eyes and yell, "The glare is back! Warn all approaching aircraft within a five-mile circumference!"

> *But it is precisely because life is so serious and the stakes are so high that we need to laugh more.*

I have explained about five hundred times that this is not even nominally funny. You'd think that after multiple years' worth of lectures they would finally get the point.

But I am holding up pretty well, considering the circumferences.

I mean, the circumcisions!

I mean . . .

Oh, these kids just make me want to tear my hair out!

14

Clothes-Minded

"Can you drive me to the mall?" Brad asked one day when he was thirteen.

"Sure," I replied, pulling on my sweater.

"What are you wearing?" he half whispered, staring at me as though I had just donned a tutu.

"It's a sweater. It's nippy outside," I replied.

"No one wears sweaters!" he complained.

"I do. And how, exactly, does it affect you if I wear one?" I said.

"I'm not going to the mall with you dressed like that!" he protested.

He was right. We did not go to the mall with me dressed like that. We both stayed home. I was just a bit happier about it than he was.

It is astonishing just how many apparel manufacturers invest millions of dollars creating clothes that no one wears except me. In a sense, I am the ultimate fashion statement. How much more exclusive can you get than wearing sweaters that "no one else" on the planet wears?

Not only do I have an entire line of clothing dedicated exclusively to me but as an extra bonus I also drive a model car that "no one else" drives. I also listen to music that "no one else" listens to. Clearly, my entire life is dedicated to the pursuit of unique oddities that serve no other purpose than to humiliate my teenagers.

> *Clearly, my entire life is dedicated to the pursuit of unique oddities that serve no other purpose than to humiliate my teenagers.*

I don't know why Brad is so concerned about what I wear, what I drive, and the fact that I listen to "Fusion Cajun Polka."

Teens get really weird about their parents. It is as though we can't do anything without causing mortal embarrassment to the very children we have sacrificed so much for all of these years.

Well, this is my life, not his. I am from a different era, I have different tastes, and it is no skin off his nose. What I do is not a reflection on him. He needs to just get over it.

Once upon a time, my kids tried to be as much like me as they possibly could. I still remember the day when Brad was in third grade and I arranged to pick him up from school and take him to lunch. He picked out his clothes: slacks, a gray blazer, dress shoes, and a tie. A shrunken office worker. He had dressed as closely as he possibly could to look like me, and he had a huge grin on his face. I will never forget that smile.

Imitating someone else is one of the highest forms of compliment. That is why it is often so difficult when we see our kids pulling back from us, perhaps dramatically so, as they seek an identity of their own. And that identity search is often reflected in clothes that could have been purchased from a shop called The Dad-Free Zone.

"What's that on your head?" I asked Brad one day.

"A visor," he replied.

"Why are you wearing it backwards and upside down? You look like a giant ice-cream scooper," I said.

"I like it this way," he said.

"But it looks ridiculous! No one wears a visor upside down and backwards," I protested.

"I do. And I'm not trying to make you wear one like this, so how is it affecting you?" he asked.

This was sounding disturbingly familiar, which only bugged me more.

"That is not how visors are meant to be worn," I argued.

"Is there a rule book about it somewhere?" Brad replied. "What if they were meant to be worn like this and everyone else has been doing it wrong all these years?"

"The point of a visor is to keep the sun out of your eyes!" I snapped.

"I like to keep the sun off my neck," he said. "Besides, it isn't hurting you."

Oh yes it was! It was embarrassing! It was ludicrous, especially when matched with the floral board shorts, the lack of socks, and the untied shoes. It was a gigantic reflection on ME! The entire purpose of this garb was to bug ME! To get on MY nerves! To have my friends whisper about ME!

(Pause for Dave to get a grip and get some perspective.)

Actually, it isn't about me. It is about Brad. This is his life, not mine. He is nearing adulthood. He is from a different era, with different tastes, and it is no skin off my nose. I need to just get over it. He is not a cookie-cutter copy of me.

This clothing thing is a tightrope, guys. I think it calls for a light touch. Clearly, clothing that is designed to offend or to create fear, such as T-shirts with foul messages or graphics, are off the table. If your kid is trying to wear that stuff, or clothes that emulate gangs or vile bands, then the issue is far deeper than fashion. There are issues of heart and character involved.

But what do you do if your kid is really a good, decent, honest, friendly person who is making good choices and simply wearing clothes that are not in your taste?

You thank God, that's what you do. And then you bite your tongue.

Man looks at the outward appearance, but the Lord looks at the heart.

—1 Samuel 16:7

‖ 15 ‖

Always and for Never

"Can we have pizza tonight?" Brad asked after walking in the door from a hard day in the sixth grade.

"No, we just had pizza," I replied.

"We *never* have pizza!" Brad complained.

"What do you mean? We have pizza all the time!" I retorted.

"I think I was in preschool the last time we had pizza!" Brad contended. "And it was made of PlayDough!"

Both of us dug into our verbal bunkers and continued firing volleys of ludicrously overstated statements at each other.

"We had pizza two weeks ago!" I snorted.

Boom!

"Two weeks is forever! Two weeks is like the last ice age! None of my friends have to wait two weeks to have pizza!" Brad huffed.

Whump!

"When I was your age, we were lucky if we had

pizza twice a year! We weren't pampered! And we had to walk to school in blizzards and hurricanes and meteor showers too!"

Kaboom!

"You forgot the swarms of locusts!" Brad added.

Bam!

"And we had to fight off the winged

> *Both of us dug into our verbal bunkers and continued firing volleys of ludicrously overstated statements at each other.*

monkeys of doom!" I retorted.

I cannot count the times we have foolishly feuded because we overstated our positions or failed to define our terms. Recognizing that we were escalating into a stupid argument that largely hinged on different perspectives instead of objective reality, I called a time out.

"Brad, let's talk rationally about this after we take a few minutes for you to admit I am right," I offered.

Fifteen minutes later...

"Brad, let's take it from the top. What did you really mean when you said we 'never' have pizza? 'Never' means 'not ever,' and that is just not true," I said.

"Well, you said we have pizza 'all the time,' and that isn't true either," he countered. " 'All the time' would mean, like, every minute of every day, even when you are sleeping."

"Well, we certainly wouldn't want to choke on pepperoni while we snored," I mused. "So, how often do you think we should have pizza?"

"Well, the way I figure it, we have three scheduled meals a day. So if you multiply three times the number of days in a week, that equals twenty-one potential pizza-eating opportunities each week.* All I am asking is ten percent," Brad explained.

"You want pizza twice a week? That's ridiculous," I replied.

"But you are still getting ninety per-cent!" Brad argued.

"I'll make you a counter offer and meet

> *If you multiply three times the number of days in a week, that equals twenty-one potential pizza-eating opportunities each week.*

you halfway. Pizza once a week. What can be more fair than splitting the difference?" I asked.

"Who gets the leftover slices? Can Mark and I take them to school for lunch the next day?" Brad asked cautiously.

"Well, to make sure they don't go to waste, I'll take them," I said.

"Go to waste? Why would they go to waste?" Brad asked, puzzled.

"Brad, Brad, Brad," I replied, shaking my head condescendingly. "Everyone knows that cold pizza is the primary food of locusts and winged monkeys of doom. You'd never make it to school."

Whenever you find yourself using words like "never" and "always" it is highly likely that you are doing something you should always never do.

---

*Yes, Brad actually did use the phrase "twenty-one potential pizza-eating opportunities each week." It was extremely hard to keep a straight face, and I was tempted to let him win the debate on that comment alone.

16

Excessive License

When I was fifteen years old the State of California was run by cruel, mean-spirited, evil legislators who hated teenagers and refused to overturn a highly discriminatory law that made us wait until we were sixteen before we could have a driver's license.

Not content with that insult, they even made us get a *permit* first, a humiliating "pretend license," which stipulated that we had to drive around for months with an "adult supervisor" (a code word meaning "your embarrassing parent") before we could drive on our own. They might just as well have bolted huge training wheels to the car so all the other drivers could better identify and ridicule us.

Our parents actually voted these people into office, which proved that there was an official conspiracy afoot to make us look stupid and treat us like children. The adults said it was for "safety," but we knew that they were just getting back at us for drinking milk directly out of the carton.

The split second after I got my permit, I barged into the house, waved it in my dad's face, and began begging to drive.

A heartless and inhuman soul, he told me I would have to wait until he finished his lunch.

"WAIT????" I cried. "I've been waiting my whole existence for this chance! Precious seconds are ticking by! My permit is yellowing with age even as you chew your food! My life is passing before my very eyes!"

"It will pass a lot faster if you don't stop sniveling," Dad muttered as he nibbled a carrot stick.

Dad was intensely into carrots when I was in my teens, not so much because he liked vegetables or needed the roughage, but because he kept trying to quit cigarettes and it helped if he could stick something in his mouth that felt vaguely like a bright orange Marlboro. Regrettably, my dad was not the most patient man in the world to begin with, and nicotine deprivation tended to exacerbate his edginess. Had I not been so blinded by my desire to drive, I would have better noticed the little tell-tale indicators of his decreased level of calm: the nervous twitching of his left eye, the tapping feet, the small stones he would crush into powder with his bare hands.

Ignoring the ominous confluence of events—a "perfect storm," if you will—my dad and I embarked on our first session.

"Let me give you a little advice before we get started," Dad began. "First, you need to understand that what you are going to be driving is basically a two-thousand-pound bomb on wheels. You have mass, weight, energy, and a tank of highly explosive fuel hurtling down a narrow strip of pavement toward oncoming traffic. The cars that will be coming at you are equally armed. If both of you are doing 55 miles an hour, when you combine your speeds, you've got two hunks of metal shooting by each other mere feet apart at 110 miles an hour. If you hit, it would be like smashing into a solid wall of iron. I don't want you or the other driver to get wiped out in a ball of flames. And no matter how careful you are, the other guy may be a reckless idiot or a drunk. You have to be completely focused and ready for anything. Driving is the leading cause of death for young men under eighteen. That's *you*, son. So the first lesson is *caution*."

"What's the second lesson?" I gulped.

"You need to be relaxed," he replied, crunching into a carrot.

Many parents were so surly and vindictive that they refused to crouch hidden near the floor of the car so that their kids could appear to be driving alone. I knew without asking that my dad was in this camp, so I didn't broach the subject. Besides, he had already refused the dark glasses and baseball cap, so I didn't feel like pushing it.

With my dad firmly buckled into the passenger seat, I fired up the engine of his pale green 1961

Chevy Impala. This was it! I was in the driver's seat! I was cool! I was diggin' it! I was looking at myself in the rearview mirror!

"STAY IN YOUR OWN LANE OR YOU'LL GET US KILLED!" Dad bellowed.

"But Dad, I only—" I protested.

"FOCUS! EYES ON THE ROAD! AND EASY ON THE GAS FOR CRYIN' OUT LOUD! THIS ISN'T THE INDY 500!" he roared, lunging at the steering wheel.

"Dad, we are still idling in the driveway," I said softly.

He took several deep breaths.

"Son, I guess I'm just a little stressed," he said, lighting up a carrot.

I did eventually learn to drive. But it was so difficult on my dad that he almost single-handedly consumed the available domestic supply of vegetable trays during those intense weeks.

Driving is now so second nature to me that I didn't give it much thought until the ominous words "driver's training" passed the lips of my boys when they were in high school.

"Driver's training?" I asked Dale. "They are still offering that in high school?"

"I don't think the rules have changed since we were sixteen," she replied.

"Is the legislature INSANE?" I roared. "They can't be allowing these . . . these *children* to drive! It is completely irresponsible! They're fresh out of preschool! Why not just hand over a 737 airliner to a class of kindergartners? I know, let's give some third graders the keys to the space shuttle!"

Brad walked in the door about then.

"Brad, your school doesn't offer driver's training to sixteen-year-olds, does it?" I asked.

"No way!" he replied.

"Oh. Well . . . good," I stammered, feeling greatly relieved.

"You can get a permit at fifteen and a half," Brad explained. "I get to sign up next week."

"Get me some carrots," I managed to mutter to Dale before I fainted.

17

Driving Me over the Edge

Once upon a time there was a father who planned to pen a short but mirthful chapter about the close calls he had while teaching his boys to drive. Unfortunately, this father had agreed, years earlier, to give his boys veto power over anything he planned to reveal in print about their lives. The father made this promise when his offspring were much younger and therefore much more trusting and innocent and gullible and easy to exploit. The father neglected to fully consider the fact that, unlike little boys who don't even care if their pants are zipped, teenage boys are *extremely* concerned about their image.

Thus the father's rash and foolish promise came back to haunt him when the subject of driving came up, because both his kids became VERY sensitive about revealing ANYTHING about these terrifying close calls, including the incident about the police officer who tailed the father and son for *miles* because from all outward appearances the car was being piloted by a severely impaired or possibly even *blind* person who was somehow holding hostage a balding and slightly overweight passenger who was clearly lunging to get out of the car even though the car was traveling at freeway speed.

So here's the compromise. I will not write about my kids' driving. I need to honor their desire for some small shred of privacy. This was a tough decision, because there is a mother lode of storytelling ore to be mined here, but that's the kind of dedicated and sensitive father I am.

I will, however, write about the *theoretical* experiences a *theoretical* father might have while attempting to teach his kids to drive. If some of these theoretical experiences appear to bear a striking and uncanny similarity to any real experience experienced by any inexperienced drivers in my household, please chalk it up to one of those wild and inexplicable coincidences you sometimes read about in the supermarket tabloids.

(For the record, both of my boys have lodged formal protests against this approach, calling it a "sham," a "dirty trick," and a "weasely way to cheat." They threatened litigation, but I pointed out that if they sue me for everything I have and force me into poverty it will be even harder for them to hit me up for money. Plus, I will no longer be able to participate in our favorite father/son bonding activity wherein I stock the refrigerator full of food and they, along with their locust-like horde of friends, strip it bare in twenty minutes. So they are really kind of stalled in their tracks.)

So let's say, hypothetically, that there was this kid who really, really, really wanted to learn to drive, but his tyrannical and oppressive father had laid down three key stipulations: a minimum of a B grade average; respectful and responsible behavior; and after attaining the proper, legal age, which in our state is thirty-two.

Well, it *should* be thirty-two.

I mean, honestly, wouldn't you feel much safer if you knew that every other driver on the road was at least thirty-two?

I certainly would.

But as we saw in the last chapter, our state vehicle code, which permits our children to drive as soon as they prove they can tie their own shoes, was authored by the same people who wrote the state tax code. So this is proof that, deep down, the legislature hates us.

Some parents balk at the state's minimum driving age and decide to wait a bit longer before they hand their children the keys. These parents understand that inexperi-

> *Some parents balk at the state's minimum driving age and decide to wait a bit longer before they hand their children the keys.*

enced young drivers can harm themselves and others. These parents base their decision on both empirical data and a gut-level sense of whether their own kids are really ready to take on this major new responsibility. These parents are honestly trying to do what is in the best interest of their kids. These parents will be viewed by their kids as the moral equivalent of the despotic heathen pharaoh who, in a clear and flagrant violation of the revealed will of God, would not set the children of Israel free.

Let's say that, theoretically, I was one of those parents. I'm not saying that I am, as this is still technically an exercise in imagination. But if I was, and if I told one of my kids he could not get his driver's permit the split second he turned fifteen and a half, just imagine the stunned expression, the sheer incredulity, the shrieking, the caterwauling, the moaning, the whining, the wailing, the begging, the sniveling, the lamenting, the whimpering, and the abject fussing that would ensue.

"But NO ONE ELSE makes their kids wait to drive! This is so LAME! I might just as well be AMISH!" a theoretical child might complain.*

At this point, a father might find it amusing to make a humorous comment about getting a new butter churn (not that I admit to anything like that).

A father may also begin clipping newspaper stories about local teenagers who seriously hurt themselves or someone else in a collision. A father may also insist that the oppressed Hebrew slave brush up on his Spanish skills and get the grades up or forget about the chariot altogether.

In response to his unimaginably horrific plight, a would-be teenage driver could end up in the following scenario, which is the driving equivalent of begging for crumbs.

---

*This theoretical child could be named Brad. In theory.

SON: "Dad, I need to take the garbage cans out to the road tonight. The garbage guys come tomorrow, you know."

DAD: "Oh. That's right. Thanks for remembering this time. We usually have to remind you."

SON: "The cars in the driveway are blocking the way. I can't get the cans by them."

DAD: "I'll grab my keys and back the car up."

SON: "PLEASE, PLEASE, PLEASE, PLEASE, PLEASE CAN I JUST BACK UP THE CAR? YOU CAN EVEN WATCH ME THE WHOLE TIME. PLEASE, PLEASE, PLEASE. I'LL NEVER EVEN LEAVE THE DRIVEWAY!"

How pitiful.

How utterly heartbreaking.

What great book fodder.

And thus it came to pass that the hard heart of the pharaoh was softened by the pitiable pleas of his groveling subject. The soul of the servant rejoiced, and there was much merriment and dancing in the driveway.

It was really pretty pathetic.

Um, I mean, were this to occur, it would be pretty pathetic.

But I remember when I was that age. I was the same way. Once I got my permit, I would beg my mom for the inestimable privilege of driving her to the grocery store. Isn't that just ironic as can be? Teenagers—the very definition of coolness and

> *And thus it came to pass that the hard heart of the pharaoh was softened by the pitiable pleas of his groveling subject.*

independence—suddenly feel an overpowering need to go everywhere with Mommy. They are reduced to gigantic toddlers, including the wailing tantrum if they don't get to go.

But back to the driveway tale.

Imagine a teenager finding joy and fulfillment and bliss in driving the car slowly up the driveway, then backing slowly down the driveway, then driving the car slowly up the driveway, then backing slowly down the driveway, then . . . you see a pattern developing.

Then imagine the day that the dad finally relents and lets the child take the test to get the permit. Then imagine the child learning on a manual transmission car.

"It really isn't complicated," the father would say. "You just put in the clutch, shift into first gear, then give it a little gas while you ease up on the clutch."

Imagine the car lurching forward ten inches and dying.

"That's OK," the dad would say. "Just give it a little more gas this time."

The trouble with the term "a little more" is that it is so relative.

Imagine the scream of the engine revving up to several billion revolutions per second. Picture the tires digging ruts into the pavement as the clutch is popped. Visualize the black smoke belching from the burning rubber as all the tread on the $400 set of steel-belted radial tires disappears in milliseconds. Imagine the dad's head snapping violently into the headrest as the G-forces press the air from his lungs.

"Stoooooooooooooooooop!" the dad would groan against the tremendous force that is starting to shove him into a different time dimension.

And imagine the father finishing lesson number one and staggering slowly into the house into which the child has already scampered. And imagine hearing the child boast to his mother, "I'm already so hecka pro at this!"

And imagine the father, with shaking hands, fumbling with the childproof lid of the Tylenol bottle, and popping two extra-strength tablets, and then lying down for a nap, thankful to be finished with the ordeal.

And imagine his son popping his head into the room and saying, "We just need thirty-nine more hours behind the wheel. So, same time tomorrow?"

Imagine the father's stunned expression, the sheer incredulity, the shrieking, the caterwauling, the moaning, the whining, the wailing, the begging, the sniveling, the lamenting, the whimpering, and the abject fussing that would ensue.

Imagine what you have to look forward to.

18

Common Scents

The Interstellar flagship Nagmanimous was patrolling the domestic quadrant when a surprise assault was launched from the Zitlot sector.

The sharp blare of the warning alarm sounded throughout the ship. The crew rushed to their stations. The soft "whump" of blast doors slamming closed throughout the ship could be heard on the bridge.

"Captain! Sensors are detecting something from the forbidden zone!" yelled the first officer. "The Zitlotians have deployed the Space Fog of Doom!"

"Red Alert," the captain snapped in reply, even as his mind raced to process the information flooding in from the sensors.

Cold fear crept up his back. Although he had personally helped negotiate the recent arms reduction treaty with the Zitlot commander, he had been uneasy with the vague terms that sealed the final agreement. If the Zitlotians had actually fired a full ampoule of the Space Fog of Doom, he would be lucky to save the crew.

As the menacing cloud enveloped the ship, he held out scant hope of survival.

"Captain! I can barely breathe!" gasped the first officer, staggering toward the living room sofa.

"Dave, it smells like Brad has just poured a gallon of cologne on himself," complained Dale, cupping her hand over her nose. "I thought you talked with him about cutting down on how much of that stuff he uses!"

"I did!" I replied defensively. "Apparently he thinks a quart is still insufficient."

"Well, let's put our foot down until he figures it out," Dale said, opening the windows to air out the overpowering scent of "Hugo" spray cologne.

"I'm venting the life-support systems and tapping the emergency oxygen supply," shouted the first officer.

"Open a hailing frequency to the Zitlot ship," ordered the captain.

"Brad! Get in here this minute! We can smell that stuff all the way down the hall even with your door closed," I barked.

The image of the Zitlot commander came into view.

"You have emitted a full dose of the Space Fog of Doom in clear violation of the Intergalactic Anti-Fragrance Abuse Treaty," thundered the captain. "My crew is barely clutching to survival. Damage assessments are off the charts. Entire planets full of innocent civilians are now at risk because of your reckless disregard of the pact."

"I only used two sprays!" Brad protested. "You and Mom always overreact to my cologne. I can barely smell it."

"Barely smell it??? Hah!" I retorted. "Did you ever notice how flocks of small birds plunge to the ground and start flopping around when you walk out the door? You are using *waaaaay* too much of that stuff. If we can smell you coming from fifteen yards away, you need to lighten up the dose."

"You leave me no choice but to launch a retaliatory strike," the captain replied grimly. "Prepare to have your ship disabled!"

"My driver's permit?" Brad asked incredulously. "You would really take away my driver's permit just because of this?"

> *"Did you ever notice how flocks of small birds plunge to the ground and start flopping around when you walk out the door?"*

"Wait," the Zitlot commander pleaded. *"The offense was not intentional! I shall make haste to engage the reverse Zimblamulator manifold and halt the destruction forthwith!"*

"I'll wash off as much as I can!" Brad promised, running down the hall to the bathroom sink.

"Subject to stringent verification standards!" warned the captain.

"See if he passes the smell test," I whispered to Dale.

Thus the crisis passed, and the known universe breathed a collective cologne-free sigh of relief. And the brave captain and first officer of the Nagmanimous again commenced their patrol of the domestic quadrant, ever vigilant for another act of malfeasance by the Zitlotians.

"Well, I think we won that round," I said gloatingly to Dale. "Let's have an ice cream sundae to celebrate."

Dale reached into the freezer, grabbed the ice cream container, removed the lid, and frowned.

"Someone ate all but two tablespoons and stuck it back in the freezer," she said.

"Dash the trickery and duplicity of the Zitlotians!" cried the captain, shaking his fist at his depleted fuel dispenser. "We shall hunt them down one by one! We shall invade their forbidden zones! We shall seize their allowance and buy some gourmet chocolate chip ice cream with caramel swirls!"

"I wouldn't open the door to his room," Dale called after me as I stomped down the hall. "That's where he sprayed on the . . ."

"Gaaaaaaah," gasped the intrepid captain as the Zitlotian trap was sprung, and he was enveloped in the Space Fog of Doom.

Tune in again next week for our exciting episode called, "The Zitlotian Fog of Doom Meets the Swirling Vortex of the Martian Commode."

‖ 19 ‖

Just Because Your Kids Are Younger, Faster, and Better Looking Than You Are, Doesn't Mean They Aren't Also Smarter

I casually peeked over the shoulder of Mark, the college student, as he sat at the dining room table rapidly working through a math problem that I promise looked exactly like this:

$$\sum \frac{P}{4nl} (R^2 - r^2)\, 2\Pi r \Delta r$$

I slowly backed away in bewildered fear, much like an indigenous Amazon native might react to his first glimpse of modern technology, such as a battery-operated nose-hair trimmer brought in by a yuppie eco-tourist.

"Don't worry, Mr. Indigenous Almost-Naked Person! I come bearing the indispensable gifts of modern civilized society! Just allow me to shove this buzzing object up your nose and demonstrate why you need a—HEY, PUT DOWN THAT SPEAR!"

I majored in journalism and political science. (Go ahead and laugh. Everyone else does.)

> *Mathematics has always been a bit of a challenge to me, in the same sense that deciphering Cantonese script has always been a bit of a challenge to me.*

Mark is taking courses like calculus and physics and quantum scary theories.

Sometimes I stare at him and wonder if he really carries my genes or if he was accidentally switched at the hospital.

Mathematics has always been a bit of a challenge to me, in the same sense that deciphering Cantonese script has always been a bit of a challenge to me.

Truth be told, I am so horrendous at math, and it is so laborious and distasteful to me, that I last balanced my checkbook during the Carter administration. I am not joking here. My version of book-keeping is to get a checking account with a massive "overdraft line of credit" and write checks until the bank tells me I have a deficit equaling that of a small third-world nation. Then I use my savings to pay off the loan, haughtily inform my bank that their services are no longer required, and I open a fresh account at a new institution. As cumbersome and complex and pathetic as this may sound, it is way easier than doing the math.

Mark actually loves math.

"It's just logic," he will say, not at all meaning to sound condescending. He just thrives on what he sees as the beauty, the precision, and the rationality of numbers and complex equations. He will occasionally make a stab at explaining a problem or theory to me, and inevitably my eyes glaze over and I slip into a coma and my wife has to call the paramedics.

"Unit Four calling Medical Central. We have a Caucasian middle-aged journalism major who has succumbed to a huge dose of algebra with complications from calculus."

It isn't that I feel intellectually inferior to Mark. To the contrary, I feel intellectually inferior *and* balding *and* overweight *and* geezerly.

It didn't happen all at once. There were slow but sure signs leading up to this point.

There was the day he was chasing me around a big field, and for the first time in my life I was actually laboring to elude his grasp—and I realized that my "little boy" was not so little anymore.

There was the day he helped his high school swim team relay squad take first place in a divisional heat—and as he climbed out of the pool (dressed remarkably like an Indigenous Almost-Naked Person), I realized that he was taut and firm and athletic and I was, um, not.

And then there was that fateful day he asked for help understanding a math problem—and it was so far over my head that I couldn't grasp it any more than I could touch Neptune.

Sure, I could still help him with his English papers. And even I could do the math on this equation: Younger, Stronger, Better-Looking, Knows-Math Person against Guy Who Can Edit Dangling Participles.

I mean, face it, it is the math guys who create space shuttles and bridges and skyscrapers. How does a wordsmith compete with that?

"Oh, sure, you math guys can design a cutting-edge air force fighter aircraft, but I dare you to crank out a press release!"

No contest.

Whoa! Was that it? Was I in a contest with my own son?

A contest for what?

(Pause while the journalism major slaps himself back into reality.)

WHACK, WHACK, WHACK!

No. I am not in competition with Mark. But I have been in a slow and inexorable slide off a pedestal for many years. It is not a pedestal I consciously mounted. It is where my son put me when he was just a tot.

Daddy is the strongest person in the world. Daddy is the fastest runner in the world. Daddy is simply the best at everything.

Kids really believe that. We know it isn't true. We know who we are. We know our weaknesses and fears and points of failure. But oh how we bask, perhaps unconsciously, in the adulation of our offspring.

And then they grow. In stature. In wisdom. In their perception of reality.

And it is hard to be seen as we are. It is hard to have them surpass us—even though we are cheering them on.

I was embarrassed the day I could no longer help Mark do his math. But I was so very proud of him. And today I delight in bragging to his grandparents about just how sharp he is in math.

But, of course, he still needs me to critique his essays.

I am also pleased to report that Mark did recently come to me with a math-related problem he did not know how to solve.

"Um, Dad, I'm afraid I got in kind of a hurry lately when I was registering for classes, and I wrote a bunch of checks I forgot to record. I have no idea how much money I have in my account. What should I do?" he asked.

"Ah, my lad, I just so happen to be an expert in this," I replied, gleefully rubbing my hands together.

Kids. They may be younger and smarter and better looking than us, but that doesn't mean we can't still teach them a thing or two.

20

The Day Everything Changed

The phone rang early. Too early.

"Hullo?" I muttered groggily.

"Dave, it's Fran."

It was the voice of my immediate boss.

My mind clicked into gear. *What day is it? Did I miss an early meeting? What's up?*

"Go turn on your television," she continued. "The World Trade Center in New York has been attacked by terrorists. The Pentagon is in flames. I'll talk to you later."

The line went dead.

I moved, stunned and disbelieving, to the living room and clicked on the television. I saw what we all saw. Again and again and again.

I walked down the hall and shook Brad awake.

"The country is under attack. Come to the living room."

I woke Mark with the same message.

Dale was already up.

We gathered around the screen and tried to take in the enormous horror that unfolded before our eyes.

Dale cried, holding her hand over her mouth.

I wanted to cry but could not. I was frozen.

Mark and Brad stared in grim silence.

What does a father do the Day Everything Changes?

The towers were smoking, but still standing. We ripped ourselves from the screen, turned down the volume, and prayed for the families of the victims, for the survivors, for the nation.

The first tower fell.

Then the second.

"This can't be happening," I said out loud.

But it was.

What does a father do the Day Everything Changes?

In my case, a father does some things right and some things wrong.

Prayer was right.

The flash of deep hatred, the wish that I had the God-like power to hurl souls into hell, was wrong.

The repentance was right.

The renewed rush of hatred was wrong.

The confession of sin was right.

Slipping into foul language was wrong.

Talking with my family was right.

Snapping at people was wrong.

Attending a prayer meeting was right.

Getting mad at several of the other people praying because I thought their prayers were shallow and foolish was wrong.

For the next several days I swung back and forth between right and wrong like a human pendulum.

The desire for justice was right.

The verbal ripping into others, and particularly the ripping into other Christian people with whom I disagreed, was wrong. I was livid at some of the

For the next several days I swung back and forth between right and wrong like a human pendulum.

things I heard other people say, and I launched scathing sarcasm like a missile barrage of words. In one heated moment I fired off an e-mail to several friends, blasting away at what I felt were stupid or harmful comments coming out of the Christian community.

Dale came into the room, scanned what I was writing, and said softly, "Dave, that is too harsh, too sarcastic, and too mean-spirited. Even if you think other people are saying things that are faulty, they will not listen to you if you just explode on them. This is not correction. This is anger."

"I don't care how anyone feels right now," I snapped, hitting the "send" button. "I'm trying to stem the flood of damaging messages that have been unleashed out there. I hope this gets forwarded all over the place."

Unlike some of the people who were spouting off theories about why God allowed it to happen, I *knew* the answer. And the answer was that evil lunatics who hated our country and our people decided to attack us. God gave people the capacity to make choices, and these fiends used that freedom to hijack jets and kill innocent people by the thousands. That was the end of it. That was the answer. Case closed. There was no mystery.

Dale knew it was fruitless to discuss it further. My righteousness had been indignated, and everyone was about to feel my wrath.

I called my best friend to vent further. And to have him confirm how right I was.

"Oh, so you are the one who has finally figured out the mystery of evil in the world?" he asked quietly. "This is something people have struggled with for centuries. We can't answer the question of why a loving God allows so much evil in the world. But we have to trust that He is still good and still loves us. What we do know is that He hates evil and will judge it. But as to why He allowed it? No one can say."

"So what are you saying? That God had some *purpose* in this?" I asked. "That line of reasoning would make Him complicit in it! Don't tell me God has some kind of purpose in this, like there is some kind of justification for it! What are you *saying*?"

"I am saying that we all need to shut up. Since God has not spoken out loud about it, we need to put our hands over our mouths. We know that God will judge evil. The people who did this will be judged. But don't try to put everything in a safe box. God is bigger than your box. We all need to shut up, and help as many people as possible, and pray, and share the gospel, and defend our nation, and stop pretending we can make sense out of it all.

God is bigger than your understanding of Him or the universe."

I slowly deflated, went back to my computer, and sent a follow-up message:

```
I want to apologize to everyone I
vented upon in my last e-mail. It
was caustic and out of line.
    I am working through my own con-
fusion about evil in the world. I
have tried to explain it to myself
in a way that seems to be rational.
But it is profoundly arrogant of me
to assume that I understand and can
wrap up in a tidy package a mystery
that has troubled saints through
the ages.
    The book of Job still terrifies
me. And I tend to lash out when I am
fearful or confused. It was not
fair. Please accept my very sincere
apology.
    Dave
```

Over the course of the next few days we talked a lot as a family. We talked about life and death. About the difference between justice and revenge. Aggression and self-defense. A just war versus an unjust war.

As each day wore on a new subject came up.

On some college campuses and in some communities, the "no violence is ever justified" crowd began holding protests. These folks seemed to believe that dialogue, understanding, and the worldwide redistribution of wealth could solve all human conflicts. Some objected to flying the flag of the United States, calling it a "symbol of oppression."

> *God is bigger than your understanding of Him or the universe.*

"I can't stand stupid people," Brad said. "Like, we are just supposed to let people blow up our cities? Why do we have to put up with these idiots? We ought to jail all the stupid protesters."

"They are incredibly naïve, Brad. But people in the United States are free to be naïve," I replied.

"And stupid," Brad added.

"That too," I replied.

And on it went.

We grappled, we talked, we reflected, we adjusted to our new world.

What does a father do on the Day Everything Changes?

He loves his family. He prays for a hurting world. He struggles with his fears and failures. He apologizes when he is wrong.

And he lives with the tension of not understanding that which cannot be understood.

> *There is a time for everything,*
> *and a season for every activity under heaven:*
> *A time to be born and a time to die,*
> *A time to plant and a time to uproot,*
> *A time to kill and a time to heal,*
> *A time to tear down and a time to build,*
> *A time to weep and a time to laugh,*
> *A time to mourn and a time to dance,*
> *A time to scatter stones and a time to gather them,*

A time to embrace and a time to refrain,
A time to search and a time to give up,
A time to keep and a time to throw away,
A time to tear and a time to mend,
A time to be silent and a time to speak,
A time to love and a time to hate,
A time for war and a time for peace.

—Ecclesiastes 3:1–8

‖ 21 ‖

A Christmas for One

The mission my wife gave me was fairly simple: Drive to the store with our two boys, Mark and Brad, and return with two strands of outdoor Christmas lights to augment our existing supply. This was another phase of her multiyear experiment in which she tried to gauge exactly how much risk she could take in sending me, and the boys, on rudimentary errands without sustaining massive economic overkill as we brought home a host of crucial items that were not on the shopping list.

Her calculations proved to be, once again, horribly flawed. You'd think she would have learned her lesson after the test in which she sent us out to buy flour and we came back with a four-person raft.

"Couldn't you have at least bought the flour *too*?" she asked.

"They were out," I replied.

"Out of flour? Dave, you went to a sporting

goods store! They don't *carry* flour!"

"Well, that explains it, then," I said.

Logic is such a rare commodity today.

> You'd think she would have learned her lesson after the test in which she sent us out to buy flour and we came back with a four-person raft.

Our family has always loved outdoor Christmas lights. From the time our boys were very young, we have taken slow driving tours of our town at night during December. We take hot chocolate in a Thermos, wrap ourselves in blankets, roll down the car windows, and cruise through the wonderland of lights.

Our own Christmas decorating began modestly enough with a few strands of lights around a couple of windows. That wasn't enough for the kids, especially when they saw how cheap the lights were the fateful day we browsed through the aisles on our shopping mission.

"These only cost two bucks for a hundred lights," Brad whispered softly, lest any other shopper notice the great deal before we could buy out the entire aisle.

"Well, I guess we could get a few more," I said.

Mark began scooping lights off the shelf by the armful.

"Um, Mark, 'a few' does not mean 'all,' " I said. "Mom actually only wants two more strands. We can probably increase that a little, but not too much."

"But they're on *sale*! We can light up our whole

house almost for free! Even the roof! And all the trees!" Mark said.

"But . . ." I cautioned.

"Plus, it would be fun!" Brad said.

The logic was unassailable.

We walked into the house carrying enough Christmas lights to illuminate a large metropolitan runway, or perhaps even a small nation.

We walked into the house carrying enough Christmas lights to illuminate a large metropolitan runway, or perhaps even a small nation.

Dale gasped.

"Why on earth did you buy all of those lights?"

"They were out of flour," I replied.

"But . . . but . . . I didn't ask you to get flour," she stammered.

"So much the better, then," I replied.

With the enthusiastic help of the boys, I began hanging several linear miles of lights while Dale took two aspirin and a warm bath.

The result was splendid. Beautiful. Breathtaking.

It was so visually stunning that we scarcely noticed the sharp whine of the electric meter as it spun with the velocity of a buzz saw. (The subsequent utility bill equaled the annual gross domestic product of Argentina. But, as Brad noted, it was fun.)

We added to the lights each year, even though Dale did not specifically request that we take on this task. On several occasions, we had to divert her attention so we could leap into the car and speed to the store before she discovered our intentions.

"Dale! Look out the back window! In the sky! Is that Haley's Comet?"

"I don't see any . . ." her voice trailed off as the car roared from the driveway.

The first year we moved to our current home, when Brad was ten and Mark was twelve, we again put up our light display. By this time we had enough wiring yardage to drape the windows, roof lines, chimney, garage, front fence, hedges, bushes, trees, and stray cats that walked through the yard. We even put up an outside Christmas tree and loaded it with all the remaining lights.

Dale could not walk outside at night without using sunglasses.

"Isn't this a little bit excessive?" she asked, hand on her brow to shield her eyes from the glare.

But our neighbor, an elderly woman named Millie, loved the display.

Millie was a widow and lived in the house across the street. She rarely left her home, largely because she looked after an equally aging relative who lived next door to her. She watched ministers on TV and prayed in her home because she would not leave her relative alone.

"I just love to see your lights!" Millie told Dale one day. "I look forward to it each year. I can't get out so much anymore, but I can look out my window and enjoy the sight. It makes my Christmas."

In fact, it was our Christmas light display that really sparked the friendship between Millie and Dale. It opened the door to conversation, and things took off from there. One of Millie's Christmas traditions was whipping up pounds and pounds of homemade candies, which she gave to friends and loved ones. She showered us with fudge, maple-covered walnuts, peanut brittle, and a broad array of the goodies that are so rare to youngsters today, but known so well to a generation that fades with the passing of each season.

"She *made* all this?" Mark asked as Dale brought in a tray Millie had given us.

"That must have been a ton of work," Brad said. "Why does she do it?"

"Because she loves to," Dale replied.

In the years that followed our introduction to our grandmotherly neighbor, Dale, Millie, and other ladies would occasionally get together for tea or a visit. And Dale would pop in on Millie now and then to chat. It meant the world to Millie just to see our kids playing in the front of her house.

But as the boys grew, developing new hobbies, friends, and interests, our annual festival of lights began to dim. The boys and I would still put up lights, but fewer of them, and sometimes just days before Christmas. Life was busy, and there were just too many other things to do. It was only because Dale kept prodding us that we kept the tradition alive.

A year finally came in which Brad said, "Let's just hang a couple of strands on the fence. We live on a dead-end street, so no one even sees it except us and a couple of neighbors. Besides, it's almost Christmas, and we'll just have to take them down in a week."

I agreed, forgetting for a moment about one old, frail, sweet person.

But Dale was now leading the charge of the light brigade.

"It's important for Millie, even if no one else sees them. Please put up everything."

So Brad and I got the ladders and flashlights and trudged out into the night.

I think one of the biggest lessons you can teach your kids is the truth that little things matter to God. And little people matter to God.

Jesus said that God notices, and rewards, small acts of thoughtfulness done in His name, even down to giving a thirsty person a glass of cold water. A glass of water may not seem like a big deal to us, but even tiny acts of service seriously matter to God.

Most of us will never be "great" as the world counts greatness. Most of us won't be in the headlines, won't be on TV, won't be in the spotlight, and won't wield great power. Odds are, most of us will scarcely be noticed outside of our small circle of family, friends, and associates.

But who we are and what we do are important to God, and no kind act will be forgotten by Him.

I think one of the biggest lessons you can teach your kids is the truth that little things matter to God. And little people matter to God.

Millie passed away in the summer of 2001. Our family was at the small graveside service, which was attended by just a handful of people.

We will continue to put up our Christmas decorations, knowing that they are a pale imitation of the dazzling display Millie is enjoying now.

22

The Lost Boy

Dale and I were at the mall, standing at the cash register of a men's clothing store and forking over some hard-earned money in exchange for some trousers. Mark was almost three years old and bored stiff, but not yet fidgeting. I let go of his hand for the ten seconds it took to open my wallet and hand a few bills to the clerk. I reached back down for Mark's hand—and he was gone.

I spun around. No trace of him.

"Dale, did you see where Mark just went?" I asked, not overly concerned. After all, he couldn't have gone far.

"Didn't you just have him?" she asked, alarmed, scanning the store.

"Excuse me," I said to the clerk.

"Mark!" Dale and I began calling as we snaked through the aisles of the small store.

It took less than thirty seconds to cover the entire store and meet back at the counter. No Mark.

"You stay here, I'll go out into the mall," I said

as a cold sweat broke out on my forehead.

"I'll call mall security and have them watch all the exits," the clerk called after me.

I looked up and down the vast aisles. No Mark.

I began running through the cavernous mall, stopping random strangers and asking if they had just seen a toddler in blue corduroy pants and a white shirt with little bears and balloons on it.

Almost everyone I stopped took one look at the panic on my face and started hunting for him.

"What's his name?" asked a couple with toddlers in tow.

"Mark. He's almost three."

They went off in another direction, calling, "Mark! Mark!"

I ran back and forth in all directions, covering as much ground as I believed Mark could have possibly covered on his own. I ran into other stores, scanned the area, and ran back out.

Nothing.

It had been five minutes, and there was no sign of him.

I made my way back to the men's store, where Dale was down on her knees, peeking under racks of clothes.

She looked up at me as I rushed back in the door.

Her face was pale.

"Not here?" I whispered, stunned.

The mall security had arrived and began taking a description. Ten minutes had now passed. Ten minutes that seemed like a millennium.

Our son was lost.

Adrenaline coursed through my veins by the gallon. I saw nightmarish visions of some creepy guy hurriedly stuffing Mark into a car. I ran the circuit of the mall again. I checked the rest rooms.

He had simply vanished without a sound and without a trace.

Could someone have been watching us earlier, just waiting for the chance? My blood turned to ice water at the thought. I ran even faster.

Fifteen horrific, agonizing minutes ticked by, and with each step I took I could feel Mark slipping away from me.

I sprinted back to the men's store.

I could barely look Dale in the eye.

The mall security guys were calling the police.

I was now insane with fear and rage. I was ready to literally kill, with my bare hands, whoever had my son. I would have traded my life on the spot to bring Mark safely home.

Every horrible kidnapping account I had ever read burned through my mind like a flame.

But there was no one to attack. No one to bargain with. No one to beg.

Every horrible kidnapping account I had ever read burned through my mind like a flame.

Each time a new person walked into the store, we looked at them with hope—only to be crushed. We told the story again and again, enlisting new volunteers.

"How long has it been?" asked yet another shopper, concern etched into her brow.

"Twenty minutes," I replied, fighting back tears.

She shuddered and began methodically probing into each circular rack of clothes.

I wanted to scream, *Don't you think we've already looked there?!* But she was only trying to be helpful.

She moved to another rack, swept back the dark slacks, and paused.

"Well, guess who is looking for *you*, young man?" she asked loudly.

We rushed to her side. And there was Mark, eyes twinkling, grinning from ear to ear. He was standing on the brace bars. You could not see him by simply looking under each rack of clothes. Clever boy. Too clever.

Dale swept him up, and we sandwiched him in a long hug and a long reprimand.

Hide and Seek.

It was a game we played all the time at home.

Mark was completely used to my walking around the house announcing, "I just can't find Mark! Where could that little boy be?" But I always found him at home.

He had no idea what he had just put us through.

It has been sixteen years since that traumatic event, but I still feel the stab of panic when I think about that day. Unless you have been through it, I don't think you can really understand the anguish of a moment like that. It slashes like a saber, right into the core of your heart.

There are many ways to lose your kids, and all of them are painful in the extreme. Parents lose their kids to disease and accidents, and even to the murderous evil of terrorists. Divorce and separation wrench kids from parents, sometimes putting so many miles between father and son, mother and daughter, you might as well live on different continents.

But there is another kind of aching loss that hovers like an ominous cloud over many parents, even if their kids live in the same town. It is the

> *It has been sixteen years since that traumatic event, but I still feel the stab of panic when I think about that day.*

loss of what could have been. What should have been.

Dale and I know parents who are deeply spiritual people, who worked and prayed for years to pass on the baton of faith to their kids. They seemed to do all the right things, teaching their kids early on about the God who loves them and wants them to be part of His family forever. They taught the Bible. They took the kids to Sunday school. Camp. Youth group. You name it.

And the kids are as spiritually lost as a needle in a field of hay.

Some of them are staggeringly successful as far as Wall Street measures success. They are rich, powerful, elite. And lost.

Some have completely messed up their marriages, blown apart their family life, and generated a police record. They are so terribly lost.

Sometimes they find their way back. It is as if they awake from a bad dream and realize they have lived the life of a fool. Sometimes they make a fresh start. The marriage is saved, the drugs are forsaken, the son comes in from the rain.

But others drift forever, cast upon the cold gray ocean of lostness, never finding the shore.

This distressing drama of lostness has played itself out again and again for thousands of years.

> *The tale of a child lost and a child found lies at the heart of what is arguably the most powerful story Jesus ever told.*

The tale of a child lost and a child found lies at the heart of what is arguably the most powerful story Jesus ever told. It is the story of a son who demands his "freedom." Who turns his back on his father, his faith, and his family. Who takes the money and runs into a life of "parties," shallow friends, and loose women. He actually thinks he is having a great time until the money runs out, the friends abandon him, the women look for a new boy toy, and suddenly he is isolated, humiliated, hungry, and scared.

So he takes that first painful step back on the path home, wondering if it is even possible that his father will allow him to work as a hired hand.

> *But while he was still a long way off, his father saw him and was filled with compassion for him; he ran to his son, threw his arms around him and kissed him.*
>
> *The son said to him, "Father, I have sinned against heaven and against you. I am no longer worthy to be called your son."*
>
> *But the father said to his servants, "Quick! Bring the best robe and put it on him. Put a ring on his*

finger and sandals on his feet. Bring the fattened calf and kill it. Let's have a feast and celebrate. For this son of mine was dead and is alive again; he was lost and is found." (Luke 15:20–24)

Jesus did not attempt to explain the allegory. He didn't have to. It is a story that can and does still reduce readers to tears. It certainly can turn me into a weeping wreck.

I do sometimes wonder if it is an actual account about a real father and son or simply a poignant story. Not that the account loses any of its intensity if it is simply a parable, because the dramatic tale is merely a shadow and copy of the true story played out in real life by God himself.

Earlier I said that if it were possible I would have traded my life to bring my lost son safely home. And I truly would have.

But Jesus actually did it.

He traded himself away to get us back.

And He keeps welcoming the lost ones home, every day, by the droves.

As long as we are still breathing, it is never too late to come home.

23

Say Again?

I opened Brad's mid-term report card and scanned the grades.

English was good.

Math was OK.

Physical education was great.

History was fine.

Spanish was . . . *failing?*

"FAILING????" I erupted at Brad. "This is absolutely unacceptable, young man! You'd better get used to not going *anywhere* on the weekends until this grade is back up to passing! FAILING???"

"Spanish is boring!" he whined.

"Too bad! It's a requirement! And you are *not* going to fail it. I'll enroll you in summer school if I have to! You'd better kiss all your extracurricular activities good-bye until this mess is fixed. No more computer, no TV, no movies, and we may even cut out potty breaks," I snapped.

"But I'll never use Spanish! It's lame! It's a totally worthless course," he protested.

If I were given miraculous powers, I would have waved my hand and Brad would have found himself deep in rural Mexico, walking dirt streets, dressed in a clown outfit, surrounded by throngs of little Mexican children and unable to explain that despite the rampant rumors to the contrary, he did not have any candy for them.

As it turned out, I didn't need miraculous powers to make this happen. I only needed to sign the permission slip so he could go on the annual mission trip with his youth group.

> *And thus Brad found himself in the heart of Mexico, stammering, "I no speako your language-o."*

And thus Brad found himself in the heart of Mexico, stammering, "I no speako your language-o."

Brad and his long-time friend Daniel were assigned the task of rounding up a bunch of kids for a week of Bible stories, games, and youth activities. What better way is there to attract kids than to have a couple of clowns walk into the neighborhood?

It worked. Brad and Daniel were immediately surrounded by scores of little kids who squealed with excitement. Knowing the language would have come in handy, Brad realized a bit belatedly. He did know a few words of Spanish—just enough to understand that the children were convinced that the clowns had come to give them goodies. But he did not know how to say, "I do not have any candy."

Daniel saw the writing on the wall and began edging away.

Brad was in the thick of the mob. He was also generously outfitted with pillows in strategic places beneath his clown suit in order to make him look portly, with a derriere the size of a Chevy. The kids began poking and prodding, and soon they were kicking Brad's immense, absurd fanny.

The ability to speak Spanish was suddenly no longer a "lame" idea.

Digging deeply into his extremely limited repertoire of foreign words, Brad suddenly motioned for silence and shouted, "Uno momento!"

The kids, startled by the command in their native tongue, quieted down and looked at Brad expectantly.

"Then I ran for it," Brad explained later. "I ran like crazy for the bus with about a hundred little kids following me."

Back at the base camp, all they saw was a sprinting Bozo followed by a big cloud of dust.

Fortunately, someone had candy.

I think going to Mexico on Easter vacation helped Brad on several levels.

As the apostle Paul once said, "I have become a fool for Christ." Paul did not dress up in a clown suit, but he did lay down a principle that says we should be willing to risk our reputations (and our coolness) to reach others with the Gospel. Both Brad and Daniel were literally clowns for Christ, and I think they will get some kind of eternal reward for it.

It was also Paul who said we are "ambassadors for Christ."

As all ambassadors know, and as Brad learned the hard way, it is a lot easier to be an ambassador if you speak the language.

Lastly, being immersed among Spanish-speaking people seemed to have one very practical benefit for Brad. He passed his Spanish class.

24

Geezer Guys

This is the poignant tale of two dads, two lifelong friends, two conversations, and the passing of two decades. Sadly, the writer is not fabricating any of this.

Years ago my roommate Tim and I used to sit around our apartment late at night discussing the nature of man, or eschatology, or some heavy spiritual tome by Charles Spurgeon, or even the seventh chapter of Romans. We would say things like this:

TIM: "So, do you think the man Paul is describing in Romans 7 is himself as an unbeliever, as a believer, or just a theoretical man cast in the first person as a rhetorical device?"

ME: "Um, not a rhetorical device. I think it is definitely personal, but I don't know how you can square the despairing language with the triumphant tone of Romans 8. It has to be past tense."

TIM: "While he was still under the law? Hmmm. I don't know. It sounds very present tense, and it squares with our experience as humans."

ME: "But since when do we measure objective truth by our personal experience?"

This would go on for *hours*.

Fast forward to a recent call from Tim, and note how our conversation reveals the subtle nuances of our maturing process:

> TIM: "Hey, my kid gave me one of those nose-hair trimmers for my birthday!"
>
> ME: "An entire appliance just to trim your nose hairs? How pathetic. Why don't you just use the sideburn trimmer that comes with your razor? That's what I do."
>
> TIM: "But then you have to hold it upside down and at weird angles. This is much more efficient."
>
> ME: "Tim, listen to us. We are talking like geezers. We used to talk about big things, important things, *deep* things—and now we are talking about the best way to remove excess hair from our nostrils."
>
> *Pause.*
>
> TIM: "Well, it works for ear hairs too."
>
> ME: "Really? I hate ear hairs. How much did it cost?"

While a surface comparison of those two conversations may make it seem that Tim and I have been transformed from keenly spiritual young men into profoundly oafish old coots, you really have to hear the rest of the conversation before you can confirm that you are correct.

Wait a minute. That didn't sound right. What I meant to say is that you need to keep listening before you come to any conclusions.

Continuing on . . .

TIM: "You know, as I get older I can understand the panic that middle-aged guys feel. It's the mid-life crisis. We are all getting older, we are sprouting nose and ear hairs, and we can actually see our youth slipping away from us. If I didn't have heaven to look forward to, I would probably panic too."

ME: "Yeah. The big yellow bulldozer of time is shoving us to the edge of eternity and there are no brakes. It all happened so fast. Life is a vapor. I don't know what I would do if I didn't have a future to look forward to beyond the here and now. Ultimately, we end up in the presence of God. That keeps me focused. It gives me hope."

TIM: "Plus, I'm in better shape than you. Do you ever actually exercise? Other than pumping forks?"

ME: "Listen, bifocal eyes, at least I'm not wearing the glasses my grandfather wore."

TIM: "Putz."

ME: "Dork."

TIM: "Dweeb."

ME: "Geek."

We then hang up.

Tim and I were in the third grade together. We went through high school together. We were in each other's wedding. Our toddlers played together in a big cardboard box in Tim and Pam's living room— a box we eventually packed with stuff as we helped them move away.

So we have grown up together, even though we have clearly never quite grown up.

Our wives are amazed at just how rapidly we revert to our junior high school mentalities when we get together—even tossing friendly insults we pull from the dusty attic of our memories.

"Just listen to them," Pam will say, shaking her head.

"I really don't know what gets into them," Dale has replied on more than one occasion.

What gets into us is simply our boyhood.

We look like men. We are husbands and fathers, and ostensibly even professionals. Tim is a college professor, for cryin' out loud. His students would be shocked.

> *The danger is when a desire to revisit the past turns into raw panic over all the roads not traveled.*

But deep down, there is a part of us that desperately wants to hold on to the days of our youth. The crazy, more carefree days of hanging out with our friends. That's why we sometimes act like, well, our kids.

That can be an innocent enough impulse, and even positive. It can be energizing. In a sort of reliving the past—in a short visit with or brief phone call to a childhood friend—we take a small vacation from the pressures of today. Innocent immaturity can be a blast, for a while.

The danger is when a desire to revisit the past turns into raw panic over all the roads not traveled. Despair over the missed opportunities. The burning desire to know what could have been, even though logic tells us it cannot now be.

I think all guys are gripped with those feelings sometimes. And that is when we have to wrench ourselves back to the present and somehow get a grip. We may even need to call that old friend and admit, "This is what I'm feeling like. Talk sense into me!"

Too many dads about my age do really stupid stuff when they panic. And they hurt their families.

Oh, and about the identity of the man in the seventh chapter of Romans? The guy who felt wretched because he was sorely tempted to do the very things he hated, and felt often unable to do the things he knew were right? I finally figured out who he is.

He's me. And he's you. We're all in this together.

So, dads, listen up for a minute. Get really close, and listen carefully. Pretend I am a very old friend giving you some heartfelt advice.

You are a dad now. You are not a little boy, nor are you a teenager. You can still play and have fun, but you are never going back to your youth. All the roads before you lead in one direction—toward tomorrow, not yesterday. Take a deep breath. Realize that you are moving slowly, but surely, toward the God who made you. He'll have questions for you when you arrive.

"Did you serve me? Did you stay true to your wife? Did you keep faith with your kids? If you messed up, did you take all possible steps to make things as right as possible? Did you repent? Did you start over again?"

Live the kind of life that, once finished, moves God to say, "Well done, good and faithful servant. Enter into the joy of your Lord."

25

On a Scale of One to Ten

I was taking an afternoon nap when Brad walked into our bedroom, clicked on the light, and asked, "Are you doing anything?"

"Yes. I am lying here changing the oil in my car. What does it look like I'm doing? Turn the light off! I'm taking a nap!" I replied.

"Since you aren't doing anything, let's talk," he said.

I could sort of understand when he did this stuff as a little kid, but he was in high school.

"I need a paintball gun," he continued.

"Good idea. Go rob your savings account and buy yourself one," I replied, pulling a pillow over my head.

"Dad, there's this new kid who visited our church, and he is trying to make new friends, and he's really into paintball. But I don't have a paintball gun so I can't hang out with him and do the stuff he wants to do," Brad continued.

"Oh, I get it!" I said, slapping my hand on my

forehead. "So this is a ministry opportunity!"

"Well, yeah," he said.

"Hmmmm. I score that one a 9.5 for creativity, but a mere 3.2 for believability. Nice try, though. I commend the overall effort. Now turn off my light," I said.

"OK, how about if you make it my birthday present," Brad countered.

"Deal. Leave," I replied.

Dale and I have long scored Mark and Brad's theatrics, escapades, manipulations, and various snivelings. Employing the official Olympic Committee tabulating system, we grade the overall presentation with a final score that takes into account a host of categories ranging from "originality" to "level of difficulty."

Sometimes the judges disagree, so we add the scores and divide by two in order to arrive at a final number.

For example, the judges had a debate over whether participation in the high school youth group summer camp, which consisted of a herd of kids and leaders on a half-dozen houseboats at Shasta Lake, should be funded by us, by Mark, or some combination thereof.

"I think you guys should definitely pay for it," Mark said. "After all, it's a church function. Plus, I'll have to give up a whole week of my vacation. And I'm mostly going because you guys said I should support my youth group by attending all the key events. So, basically, it would be like forcing me to spend *my* money for something that *you* want!"

"I give that a 2.6 on the convincing scale, but

about a 9.8 for audacity," Dale said dryly.

"Actually, he's right, hon," I said to Dale. "We did tell him he needs to support his group. Let's pay for it."

"Maybe we shouldn't make him go," Dale mused. "Think of all the suffering he would experience out on that houseboat with all his friends. Why, he might be traumatized by not getting to do his chores every day. And he runs the real danger of getting a tan while he water-skis. What if the girls don't like blond guys with tans?"

"How about if you just pay half?" Mark pleaded.

"He caved too fast," I noted. "I'm only giving him a 3.7 on the endurance scale."

We gave him an overall rating of 5.6, and ninety bucks.

The real beauty of the scoring system is that it lets them know that you know that they are trying to manipulate you, but it also makes for some very interesting conversation and entertainment. Sometimes the sheer brilliance of the attempt is worth the entire price of admission.

Mark barged in the house one day and exclaimed, "This is Kyle's one day off in, like, forever, and we want to go do something! I'm broke! Can you give me an advance on the lawn mowing?"

"I already gave you an advance, and so you already owe me a lawn mowing," I replied.

"Oh. Um, could I have another advance?" he asked.

"It seems to me that if you had mowed the lawn this morning, like you said you would last week, you would not need to be asking for another advance," I said, unmoved by his plight.

"I got behind," he said, grimacing.

"That's funny. I heard you playing your guitar all morning," I replied.

"OK. It's my fault," he admitted, biting nervously on his lip.

"Well, why should I reward you for blowing off your job?" I asked.

"I really was going to do it later today," he said. "But I didn't think Kyle was going to call."

"That's why you should always get your chores done before you play," I said.

Mark heaved a big sigh.

> *While consistency can be a good thing, I am also a big believer in flexibility—and grace.*

"Dad, I already know all the things you are going to say about responsibility and so on and so on and so on. I *know* the moral of the story. But watch this," he said.

He then placed his hands on his cheeks, pulled downward so he had these pitiful basset hound eyes, and began whimpering like a puppy.

It was hysterical. It was creative. And really, it was a moment that called for mercy more than law.

While consistency can be a good thing, especially when kids are younger, I am also a big believer in flexibility—and grace.

This is, again, one of those fine lines we walk as parents. You have to figure it out as you go. No one can tell you exactly when to stick to the rules and when to bend them.

When you do exercise grace—when you extend a favor that the recipient truly did not have coming to him—that can be a teaching moment. You can even say, "This is grace. You *know* you don't really deserve this break. But here you go anyway."

I have found that when Dale and I do something special and unexpected for the boys, we are often pleasantly surprised in return.

Tonight when we got home from an evening engagement, we walked into the house and found that someone had cleaned up the kitchen for us. It wasn't assigned. It wasn't required.

It was grace.

I was tempted to score it a perfect 10, but grace is immeasurable.

26

And Now a Word from Our Sponsor

Note: The following chapter is brought to you by my wife, Dale, the occasionally patient and often mortified love of my life. Because of certain "equal time" requirements that appear in the code of federal regulations, the publisher is mandated by law to include a one-chapter response by my wife. This is kind of like when the president gives a one-hour address and the minority party gets five minutes to make a fuss. So, here you go:

Of all the other parents on the playground that day, only my husband was behaving like a six-year-old.

We were on vacation in Southern California, visiting family. We had left my sister's lawnless condo complex, secured behind locked iron gates, and took the kids out to a neighborhood park to escape the concrete.

Our kids scampered up the slides and joined the

throng of other children in all colors and accents. As was the norm in our hometown playgrounds, Dave began chasing Mark and Brad through tunnels, down slides, and over tractor tires worn smooth by the touch of thousands of young hands.

A hushed awe fell over the other children. They stopped playing. Their eyes grew wide. Their mouths gaped open. I don't think they had ever seen a grown man play like one of them. They had no idea what to make of it.

There were other dads at the park, mostly sitting in their cars or killing time on benches. Most were not to be found. One macho dad observed but kept his distance.

Slowly, one after another, a stream of little boys asked, "Can you chase me too?"

"Sure!" Dave replied.

Their hesitation gave way to smiles as Dave became the largest playground playmate they'd ever had.

Like a character in a grade B mummy movie, Dave lurched stiff-legged, arms outstretched, roaring and chasing but never catching the squealing, laughing children.

It was so romantic.

Romantic?

Yes, romantic.

Typically, we think of romance as flowers, dinner out, walks on the beach, special gifts and cards, and of course, chocolate. And no sane woman is going to turn any of this down. But these are not everyday occasions. We don't expect them to be.

Those special events are meant to make us feel

appreciated and more connected, but I think husbands may not realize just how much little things they do (like taking time to play with the kids, or fixing a leaky faucet) are downright attractive to us.

At the end of the week a wife feels much more romantic toward her husband if he meets all the little needs that have been nagging at her. Women can't resist a man who fixes that annoying little broken thingamajig on the watchchamacallit. It isn't bugging anyone else, but we want it fixed. And when you fix it, we can't help but show our appreciation. It is, in fact, romantic.

> *Typically, we think of romance as flowers, dinner out, walks on the beach, special gifts and cards, and of course, chocolate.*

Typically I cook the meals and clean up the kitchen. Dave does a lot of laundry. And whenever we have a large group of company over for dinner, Dave goes into the kitchen without being asked and washes the dishes and cleans up the counters.

I hear so many women say, "I hate asking." It is just easier for them to do it themselves. These husbands have no idea what they are missing.

But far more important than oiling a squeaky hinge or washing a sink full of dishes, women *respect* a man who is "there" for his family. What does it mean to "be there"?

Changing diapers. Rocking your baby late at night when Mom is exhausted and the baby has colic. Telling bedtime stories. Coming to the school play. Carving out time for the soccer game or swim meet. Taking the kids on overnight trips.

When a dad spends time building a relationship with his child, it affirms that everything his wife is doing really matters.

Affirmation makes a woman feel valued. And without this kind of practical, day in and day out "being there," all the flowers and candles and gifts are hollow.

But the combination? Wow! She won't be able to keep her hands off of you.

27

The Quest for Truth

One day at the age of four, Mark did a quick survey of our home and came to the conclusion that there was no way Santa could break in with his bag of Christmas gifts. Here is a verbatim account of the conversation Mark had with his mother. She couldn't forget it if she wanted to. Trust me, she has tried.

MARK: "Mom, we don't have a chimney. How can Santa get in our house?"

DALE: "He could come through the door."

MARK: "You always lock the doors at night."

DALE: "He could come through the window."

MARK: "We have those lock things so the windows only open a little bit."

DALE: "He could come down the heater vent."

MARK: "He would get stuck. It's too small."

DALE: "He could find another way."

MARK: "There is no other way. And he wouldn't have time to stop at all the houses. I don't think there is a Santa. I think adults invented Santa to make their kids behave."

This conversation really happened. When he was still in preschool! Mark was a hard-bitten, cynical skeptic before he hit kindergarten.

He continued the grilling with me.

"Dad, is there really a Santa?"

I tried a deft trick, explaining that historically there was a person called Saint Nicholas who was known for his generosity, etc.

Mark pressed the point.

"But is there a Santa right now? Not just someone who took over for him, but the 'zact same Santa that started out. If you say yes, and then there isn't one, I won't believe in God either," he said.

Sometimes Mark was so sharp he almost scared us. No wonder his preschool teacher was all twitchy.

> *I don't think there is a Santa. I think adults invented Santa to make their kids behave.*

"OK, here's the deal," I said. "There really was a Nicholas. He has been gone for many years. So we have kept his story alive through playing and pretending. Santa is pretend, but it is all for fun. It is make-believe. Most kids like make-believe, even if you don't. But God is real. He is not pretend. He isn't a story. But don't tell your other friends about Santa, because it is fun for them. And don't say anything to Brad!" I cautioned.

Mark seemed to accept this.

As December wore on, we found ourselves at the preschool Christmas musical, squished into tiny chairs with dozens of other parents and grandparents. We were decking the halls with camcorders and cameras. The kids were up on a platform, little construction paper antlers on their heads, belting out cute song after cute song. I had a tense moment when they began singing "Santa Claus Is Coming to Town," but Mark joined in with gusto and did not make any contrary announcements. Looking at his lips, it appeared that he *may* have been singing, "Santa Claus *Ain't* Coming to Town," but I can't be sure. If he was, no one could hear him in the din.

The show ended, the parents erupted in thunderous applause, and we were all invited to have punch and cookies. I hovered near Mark, making sure loose lips didn't sink anyone's Good Ship Lollipop.

The evening was nearly done and I actually thought we were home free when the teacher, Mrs. Pat, called out, "Children, we have a special visitor!"

In the door burst jolly old Saint Nick himself.

"Santa!" squealed two dozen children.

In the stampede that followed, Mark escaped my grasp.

"IT ISN'T SANTA!" my son called above the hubbub of gleeful children. "IT'S JUST SOMEONE'S DAD DRESSED UP LIKE SANTA!"

"Mark!" I called after him, diving over desks and assorted relatives in an attempt to rein him in.

"DON'T BELIEVE HIM! HE'S A FAKE!" shouted the apostle of holiday truth.

"Mark!" I called again, lunging at him but missing him by inches.

"LOOK! HIS REAL SHIRT IS STICKING OUT! PULL DOWN HIS BEARD! IT'S ONLY A

DAD!" Mark implored the deceived masses.

"Dave, stop him!" Dale whispered, mortified.

Mark was clearly exasperated at the sheer gullibility of his little flock. With the passion of a prophet, he took a deep breath and shouted, "*THERE IS NO SANT...*"

Like a professional outfielder for the New York Mets diving to the ground to intercept an errant ball, I lunged for Mark, caught him, and whisked him to home plate before he caused a riot among the parents.

Mark has always demonstrated a pretty strong empiricist streak.

When he lost his first tooth, we told him to put it under the pillow and the tooth fairy would leave a dollar. He agreed without argument, but I think he only acquiesced because he wanted the money.

In the morning, after safely depositing the loot in his Cabbage Patch Kid bank, he asked for his tooth back.

"I want to study it when I get older," he said.

Ah, the joys of innocent youth.

Brad, on the other hand, loved to live in the world of make-believe. He wore a Santa hat—in July. He regularly donned a suit of plastic "armor," complete with a fake saber, which he bravely thrust at the cartoon dragon on the TV screen. Brad wore a cape almost every day, and he was forever rescuing someone in distress or avenging a dastardly deed.

Although Mark was willing to watch the *Sleeping Beauty* cartoon along with Brad, only stern parental warnings prevented him from leaning over to his little brother and whispering, "It isn't real."

We have the DNA evidence to prove that Mark and Brad are related. But as I said earlier, they were very, very different people from day one.

Mark was in first grade when he announced to his mother, "I don't believe in God."

To her credit, Dale took the statement in stride and probed him to see what he was thinking.

"Do you mean that you don't believe that there is a God?" she asked.

"Well, I believe He is there," Mark said. "But I don't like Him because He lets kids starve."

Dale was taken aback. So was I when she told me about it later that day. Frankly, we had often wrestled with questions of this nature. So have millions of other people through the millenniums. But we never thought we would have this kind of discussion with our six-year-old.

We think Mark's feelings were prompted by an advertisement he saw in a magazine. The ad featured a photo of a hungry child, and explained that for a nominal amount of money per month we could help feed and clothe children in poor nations. Brad was instantly enthused about the prospect of helping, and we became contributors to the cause of helping poor kids.

But while Mark was also eager to help, he was thinking on a deeper level: since God is all-powerful, why doesn't He just fix this problem? The fact that God allowed this kind of awfulness made God seem mean and uncaring.

So we had a long conversation with Mark. We pointed out the sad reality of the fall of man, and the introduction of suffering, pain, disease, and all manner of woe in the human condition. We talked about the evil of certain political regimes who deliberately use food deprivation as a weapon to control their own people. We talked about Jesus' coming to our world, and how He suffered terribly. We talked about how He conquered death but warned us that this will be a troubled planet. We talked about a world gone wrong that will only ultimately be healed when God wraps up history. But in the meantime, God wants us to do acts of goodness and kindness in His name.

That discussion did not answer all of Mark's questions. It did not answer all of our *own* questions. But it helped.

Mark shifted his focus from blaming God to wanting to help others.

Still, Dale and I were astonished at how Mark's mind worked. He kind of spooked us.

Brad made a profession of faith very early in his life. Mark took his time. Lots of time. Years of time.

Mark was a junior in high school, filling out an application to go on the youth group mission trip to Mexico, when he got to a page that asked for a one-paragraph statement detailing "how you came to faith, why you believe."

He wrote a page. Then another. And another. And another.

It took about five pages for him to explain that he dabbled at Christianity for many years, but that he did not make a heartfelt, serious commitment to God until he saw real change happening in the lives of other students in his youth group.

It made him question his own relationship with Christ.

It prompted him to finally pray—and pray seriously—while on the "houseboats" youth group event a prior summer.

It was now his own faith, not simply the faith of his parents.

And that is how faith must always be.

Back when Dale was pregnant with Mark, when it seemed like she had been preg-

> *Parents don't want to be patient. We want to be in control.*

nant *forever* and that it would never end, the doctor kept telling her, "Don't worry. When the time is right, the time is right. Be patient."

Parents don't want to be patient. We want to be in control.

But whether it is birth or new birth, we are not in charge.

We don't pick our kids' personalities. We don't command their thoughts. Our kids are not merely extensions of us.

As parents, there is much we control, and much that is painfully out of our hands.

Early in their lives, we can control a lot. We can dress them how we want. We can make them eat strained carrots as long as we are willing to get sprayed with about half the jar. We can put them down for naps. We can teach them. We can expose them to truth, and beauty, and goodness. We can take them to church, put them in a youth group, and make them do their homework.

We can cultivate an atmosphere conducive to faith, we can model faith, we can encourage faith.

But we cannot exercise it for them.

When the time is right, it is right. Be patient.

28

The Syndrome

Dale keeps bursting into tears these days. I'll do something completely innocuous, like open a jar of olives, and the tears will flow.

"You were saving these?" I'll ask, bewildered.

"The kids are grown up," she'll sniff. "Mark is in college. Brad can drive himself wherever he needs to go. He's always gone with his friends. I'm not ready for the empty nest."

"Dale, perhaps you didn't notice that Mark is still *living here* and commuting to college. Brad has another *year* of high school to go. If this is an empty nest, I'd hate to see a crowded one," I grouse.

More tears.

"You just don't understand," Dale will weep. "I have been investing so much of my life into raising the boys, and now they are just . . . just . . . just . . ."

"Just still here!" I exclaim as Mark pops in the door, dumps half a box of cereal into a mixing bowl, inhales it, and blows out of the room.

"You're running low on granola," Mark reminds me as he trots out the door to swimming practice. In two hours he will come home starved.

Then I'm the one in tears.

This is so unfair. My wife is emotionally distraught over an empty nest that isn't empty, I can barely shovel food into the kitchen fast enough to keep stoking the adolescent steam engines we have for offspring, and to add insult to injury, Brad just swiped my olives.

"Dale, you can't have your *empty nest syndrome* when we don't have an empty nest yet," I pleaded with her one day. "There is no such thing as a *still-in-the-nest-and-costing-you-a-fortune syndrome*, unless our entire life has been a syndrome and no one told us. I am fully prepared to support your syndrome a couple of years from now when the kids are actually gone, but you can't keep bursting into tears every time we sit down for dinner and one of the boys says, 'Please pass the salt.'"

It is no use. Every time the boys do something, no matter how mundane, it is a painful reminder to Dale that someday they won't be here to do it. And the tears gush like Victoria Falls.

Fortunately, Dale can still manage to occasionally get bugged at the kids. So we have a limited reprieve from the still-in-the-nest-and-costing-you-a-fortune syndrome. But these little episodes of impatience usually occur on a predictable monthly basis, and she'll get kind of snippy for no good reason.

"Whatever that thing is that you keep doing with your eyes, you can just stop it!" she snapped at Brad one day.

"It's called blinking," Brad replied defensively.

"Well, it irritates me," Dale said.

Doesn't this just beat everything? Irrational PMS incidents are the only way I get a break from the tears associated with the still-in-the-nest-and-costing-you-a-fortune syndrome.

I have been reduced to *looking forward* to PMS.

How pathetic. I have been waiting my entire married life for things to get easier, and it never happens! Everything has always been difficult!

Pregnancy was hard. I had to go to all those classes and watch scary videotapes of the birthing process so I could be better prepared to be terrified.

Then the day finally came for the real birth—a day filled with hours of puffing, sweating, and sharp pain. And that was just filling out the insur-

> *How pathetic. I have been waiting my entire married life for things to get easier, and it never happens!*

ance forms. Labor was no cakewalk either. Admittedly Dale had a bit rougher of a workout than I did. But it was still traumatic, and they made me wear ill-fitting surgical garments. So I certainly did my share of suffering.

Then we got home with our baby, who had glaring deficiencies in his personal hygiene habits. I would be changing his diaper, and he would pee on me. Like what he had already done in his diaper wasn't bad enough? I still have scar tissue in my windpipe from inhaling fumes so toxic that the cute Noah's ark wallpaper border in Mark's room peeled off and disintegrated before my eyes.

Then there were ear infections. I spilled *gallons* of that pink liquid antibiotic as I attempted to get just one teaspoonful down Mark's throat. I could have made *millions* at the New York Gallery of Modern Art if I had simply stuck a canvas in front of Mark as he sprayed that stuff out of his mouth with the force of a fire hose.

> I have lost wads of hair, and I still wake up with night sweats over the little "learning episode" Brad had with the cigarette lighter.

Then there was the day when Mark was three and Dale and I were walking out of the house to take him to Grandma and Grandpa's so we could go out to dinner and exchange actual adult words, and he reached down on the ground, picked up a mushroom he found growing in the grass, and popped it into his mouth. I beat the Indy 500 speed record as I drove like a madman to the hospital. They gave Mark a medication to make him barf, which he did. He was the toddler version of Old Faithful. I still owe Dale that dinner out.

Bringing Brad home from the hospital took us back to square one, poopwise, just when Mark was becoming a whiz (so to speak) at bathroom duty.

We were never cut any slack.

As the kids got older, well, you've read about a lot of it already. I have lost wads of hair, and I still wake up with night sweats over the little "learning episode" Brad had with the cigarette lighter. I can't go into the details or I may curl up in a fetal position and never come out from under my blanket.

Pick up my first book, *The Hair-Raising Joys of Raising Boys,* and you'll gain an even fuller appreciation for the sacrifice, the giving, the toil, the pain, the bellowing, the twitching, and the involuntary spasms whenever anyone sneaks up behind me and whispers the term "parent/teacher conference."

Frankly, I'm ready for the empty nest! I'm ready for the days that Dale and I can just pack up and go on a spontaneous trip without having to worry about the kids. I relish the thought of having the bathroom to myself! I want to be able to walk around the house in my underwear! I want the pleasure of opening a box of crackers and finding more than fourteen ounces of air and a few small puffs of cracker powder inside.

Do the math! EMPTY NEST = FULL REFRIGERATOR.

Let 'em move out! I don't mind having my life back!

At least, that's what I tell myself when I start getting
depressed.

Sometimes I even make myself believe it for a few minutes, because I don't want to face just how hard it is going to be. Dale is weeping because she is the brave one. She is facing reality. I'm spending a lot of time and energy trying to laugh it off.

It really is harder on Dale, because so much of her identity in life has revolved around being a mom. She baked cupcakes for school events. She helped in vacation Bible school. She took the kids to parks, parties, and all manner of outings when I was at work. She poured so much of her life into theirs. So her sense of impending loss is especially sharp.

But I'm a close runner-up.

To even speak of "getting my life back" after the boys move out is ludicrous on its face. My life has been *our* life.

I can't even imagine who I would be apart from the word *dad*.

As parents, we often start out with a pretty good grasp on the general concept that God wants to use us to mold and shape our kids. We are much slower to pick up on the fact that God is also using our kids to mold and shape us. This is God's compassionate conspiracy.

It is in bringing children into the world and into our lives that God sets the stage for innumerable opportunities for patience, generosity, kindness, courage, loyalty, and sacrifice. This is for all of our sakes—Dad, Mom, and kids.

We love them and teach them to love and are loved by them.

Yes, I have molded the lives of my sons. But they have also dramatically changed my life.

I am a better human being for having been given the inestimable privilege of being a dad.

Mark, Brad, Dale—thanks for the gift.

29

The Next Adventure

Let me leave you with a few parting thoughts.

The day will come, in the not-too-distant future, when our children (and yours) will finally, actually, officially, permanently, and irrevocably leave home. This is the way it is supposed to be. This is God's plan. We will be left with a host of memories, photos, and crayon works of art we have been saving for years.

We will miss our kids, we will cry, and we will adjust to our new relationship with them. It won't be easy, but we will make it.

I don't know what the future holds for my sons. I have hopes and dreams for them, but God has not given me a glimpse into the future. I commit them to His grace.

One thing I do know with the bold assurance of a prophet: Dale and I will soon embark on an exciting new adventure in our life. We may meet you on the journey.

We will be donning our pith helmets, packing

our supplies, and taking a safari through the dangerous and completely uncharted land known as *menopause*.

It is a land of dramatic fluctuations in temperature, rivers of emotion, volcanoes of hot flashes, gales of cold sweats, shiploads of chocolate, and pits of completely irrational despair. We have nontransferable, nonrefundable, one-way tickets.

Please excuse me for a moment while I sob great wails of grief.

"Waaaaaaaaahhhhhhhh!"

Like I said before, it never gets easier. It gets different, but not easier.

God never promised us smooth sailing through the seas of life. He only promised to be with us in the boat.

Bon voyage!

Dave Meurer is the father of two sons and the author of several nonfiction books, including *The Hair-Raising Joys of Raising Boys*. He lives in northern California.

Dave Meurer can be reached at www.davemeurer.net

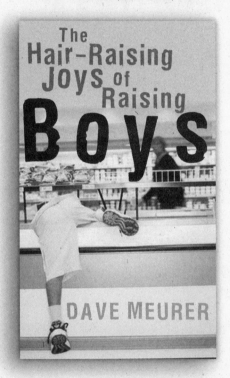